"AN AUSSIE GOES TO AMERICA"

Raymond Low
*A Memoir*

ISBN: 978-0-9910923-9-0

An Aussie Goes to America
Copyright © 2019
Digitally Reproduced by Converpage
Scituate, MA 02066

## INTRODUCTION

I have written this memoir not because I believe that my life has been of greater importance than any other but rather because I have always been curious about the lives of my forbears, and from whence they came. Apart from fragmentary memories of grandparents I knew little of the long line from which I had descended or about what their daily life was like "back then", anyone who might pick up this memoir at a later time may well find many of the events and customs found here to be quaint or even strange as the world moves on. The research of my cousin Carol Morgan and my niece Beverly Pearson has filled in some of the details, of our very early family history.

As to our Cornish roots, I remembered as a child, my grandmother Annie Walker, sending food parcels to our family in Cornwall who were in dire need after World War II.

## BEGINNING IN CORNWALL

Our family roots on the maternal side of my family go back to Cornwall in England to 1606, to a William Vines in the picturesque town of Lostwithiel which was at one time capital of Cornwall. There are still Vines' in Lostwithiel and St. Winnow. Of specific interest was William Nichols Vine who was born in Lostwithiel in 1838 and married Caroline Wellington in 1855 at St. Winnows. St. Winnows is a 12th century church in a very picturesque hamlet, sitting in farmlands and situated on the River Fowey. Caroline could not read or write so she signed with a cross, which was not unusual in the period. In 1865, they boarded the sailing ship "Chatsworth" with their four children, all under the age of ten. It took them three months to reach their destination of Melbourne in Australia. Why they left beautiful Cornwall we have no record of, but employment was hard to find and it was the news of the Australian gold rush in Ballarat that probably drew

William to undertake this arduous journey with his family. Tin mining was depressed in Cornwall at the time and as a miner, the gold rush sounded very appealing. On reaching Melbourne they travelled inland to the rich gold fields of Ballarat where fortunes were being made. One huge nugget which was fittingly called "Welcome Stranger" and weighed many hundreds of ounces, was found by another miner. A replica of it is still on display in a Melbourne museum. It was in a tent on the gold fields where my grandmother Annie Walker Melinda Vines was born in 1867.

My niece Beverly Pearson has done considerable research on the paternal side of our family. I will begin with Bridget Mahoney. It came as a complete surprise to me that I had Irish ancestors, as I had surmised we were of English descent, as we are on the maternal side. Bridget lost her father during the dreadful Irish Potato Famine. She was placed in an orphanage in Cork, even though her mother was still alive. At age 16, Bridget along with 195 Irish orphans were sent on the sailing ship "Elgin" to Adelaide Australia. It was 1849 and it took the ship 3 months to arrive in Australia. It must have been a frightening experience, a long sea journey with storms, being so young, and to arrive on a continent where she knew no one.

She was to eventually marry Abraham Leighton and she bore several children. One of them, Edward Leighton, Sr., was my great grandfather. There are copies of documents available for anyone interested.

# AUSTRALIA

William Vines was unsuccessful in his search for gold as far as we know. If he had been, those who followed him probably would have inherited a fortune. After a time, he moved to Melbourne with his family and we do not know what his occupation was there. In 1886, his daughter, my grandmother, Annie Melinda Vines, whom as I wrote was born in a tent on the gold fields, was married to Louis Alexander Walker who had been born in Hobart in 1866. They had 12 children - a lot for today but not that unusual at that time. My mother, Lillian May was born in 1901, was the 9th child in the family. She married my father, Edward Leighton in 1923. Mavis Maude, my foster mother, was the youngest of the 12 children. She was born in 1909. Grandma Walker was barely 5 feet tall and had remarkable energy and stamina. In her 70's and 80's she would travel all over Melbourne visiting her remaining nine children and their families and was the connecting link between them. Although on a pension, every visit she would slip 2 shillings into my hands, which was not an insignificant amount for her.

## EARLY YEARS

I was born in Camberwell Victoria Australia in 1931. My mother Lilian Walker Leighton died of septicemia a week later, at the age of 29. My father Edward (Ted) Leighton was left with a week old baby, a daughter Valda (4) and another son Don (2). Having lost his wife, he had no means of taking care of such a young family and to continue to work at his job on the railroads. A family conference was convened and it was decided that my mother's younger sister, Mavis, then in her early twenties and single, would adopt me and she and my Grandmother Annie would take care of me. My siblings, Don and Valda, would be cared for by my paternal Grandmother (Durling), and her husband in their home in Burwood, Victoria. When I was three, Mavis married Roy Albert Low, a master plumber and WWI veteran. They later moved to Richmond, an inner suburb of Melbourne and the scene of my boyhood memories. Richmond had become a working class inner suburb of Melbourne. In earlier days it had been a fashionable place to live for the well to-do, who had then moved out to farther away suburbs.

While I was in the second grade there was a polio epidemic, infecting hundreds of school children. All schools were closed for 6 months, and sometimes lessons were mailed to our home to try to keep us up to speed. At that time we were living in the depression years before the beginning of World War II. Families were struggling to survive and could not afford to have more children. Hence, I had few playmates. I was also beset by many childhood illnesses, including pneumonia and whooping cough and even suspected of having psittacosis, a disease caught from parrots. We had a talkative, native, white sulphur crested cockatoo and it was thought that he could be the cause of my symptoms, which turned out not to be the case. Our cockatoo had learned to mimic my mother by calling out "dinner is ready". I would come in to the house, only to be told by my mother "no it's not ready, and I didn't call". Old Cockie had fooled me again.

Around 12 years old, wanderlust had struck me, and I would catch a train, usually alone, and go to the end of the line in the country around Hurstbridge or Heidelberg, some 30 miles away. Those places are now built up suburbs. On my return home I would not reveal my journeys to my unsuspecting parents, who would not have approved, even though the times were much safer then with a low crime rate and violent crime was very rare. My friends and I thought nothing of going to the city as youngsters to attend a movie. A Christmas gift of a bicycle at 13 meant that I could now pedal my way to new places. One place that I rode through with much trepidation, was the neighboring town of Collingwood. Richmond and Collingwood were bitter football rivals and disliked each other intensely. On my way to a small waterfall I would have to go through Collingwood, and did I speed through it. We could not afford a telephone like most of our neighbors and my father never owned a car.

When I was a 12 years old I decided that I would like to sell newspapers for pocket money, without telling my parents.

The pay was four pennies for every dozen newspapers you sold. To get into a movie theatre was six pence with one penny for a treat. I had a street corner spot and I would jump on a tram to get a sale. The conductors were seldom pleased. One time I jumped off backwards and landed flat on the ground. One evening my mother happened to see me on the corner and made me quit.

North Richmond where we lived fared somewhat better than South Richmond where people struggled to put food on the table, and often 6 or more people lived in a 2 bedroom house. A large number were unemployed, alcoholism afflicted more than a few, and gangs fought over their turf. The state government neglected the inner industrial suburbs in favor of the better off outer ones.

As a kid I was quite fanatical about the Richmond "Tigers" who played in the Australian football league. "Australian Rules" as it is called is unique to Australia.

Perhaps a mixture of rugby, soccer and gridiron, played without padding, and before crowds sometimes reaching eighty thousand and more. I would travel all over Melbourne suburbs to watch an away game.

Like almost every Melbourne schoolboy we played it right through our school years and beyond.

When I came home from a Richmond game my mother would take one look at my face and say "They lost today, didn't they?"

Primary schools in Australia then were basically the 3 R's, with little or no extras, except for compulsory sporting activities after the 3rd grade. Boys and girls were placed in separate classrooms for reasons unknown to us. Central school only went to the fourth grade so I had to transfer to Yarra Park in East Melbourne for the 5th and 6th grade. Once again there were separate classrooms for girls and boys. Something that happened right through my schooling. Probably some educational guru believed this was the best way to promote learning. Socially it was not beneficial, making for awkward interaction between the sexes. Teachers were very strict, talking was not permitted and we sat all day in rows of desks. The size of the classes were large, averaging around thirty. The teachers were usually dedicated, but no extra help was offered during or after school hours. There was no P.T.O. or other parental input. It was either sink or swim. Discipline was strict. I remembered being pulled out of a line for pushing another student, and having a teacher wielding an 18" long 1/8 inch leather strap, raising it above his head and striking the palm of my hand, which stung. Six cuts as they were called was the maximum allowed. Some of the less competent teachers often used the strap to keep order, others never.

When I was 14 my stepfather, Roy, had a massive heart attack (coronary thrombosis). When he was 19, in 1915, he had joined the Australian army in the fight again Germany in World War I. He was sent with his unit to the bloody battlefields of France where thousands of men were dying almost daily. The trauma of trench warfare in this dreadful war must have been devastating. The use of poison gas added to the incredible suffering. Dad was injured in some way of which he never spoke. He was sent to a hospital in England in 1918 before being returned home to Australia.

The Australian army suffered more casualties on a per capita basis than any other allied country in the war. April 25th is forever marked in the identity of every Australian. It is Anzac Day, standing for the Australian and New Zealand Army Corp., which landed, along with their allies, on the shores of Gallipoli in Turkey in 1917 during World War I. It was one of their bloodiest defeats. Many books and films recount its history.

Every year it is remembered by a parade of veterans through Australia's capital cities. I recall vividly how as a young boy, my father would pin his combat medals to my chest and send me off to the parade. He never went himself.

When I came to Boston, the Australian and New Zealand expats, living in Boston, asked me for many years, to conduct a remembrance service at various churches on the twenty-fifth. Such is the strength of the tradition.

The Veteran Affairs agency certified dad's illness was a result of his service in France. At age 45 he was classified as totally and permanently incapacitated. From that time on he was mostly confined to home for the next 10 years. He suffered many painful times. My mother, Mavis, was his nurse day and night. She herself rarely left home except to shop for the necessities. It was a rather sad environment for a teenager to grow up in.

They had kept from me the fact that I was adopted and at the few extended family gatherings my sister and brother were passed off as my cousins, even though they knew differently. It was a huge family secret, even though my grandmother and aunts and uncles disagreed with it. Mavis, many years later, told me that Roy was afraid that I would want to go live with my biological father and siblings if I knew. Something that I would never have done.

Richmond had only one secondary school. A technical school preparing students for entry into various trades. There was a high school in a neighboring town, but transportation would have been a problem. When a student graduated from 6th grade, he/she had to decide whether to go to a high school or a technical school. At that age how would you know which was best for you? In any case parents usually made the decision. My foster father, being a master plumber, was hoping that I would follow in his footsteps, despite my lack of aptitude in this area. So it turned out I was getting 40% for woodwork, 45% for sheet metal class, 55% for motor mechanics, but 90% for English, 92% for social studies and history. Despite this I enjoyed the school, playing on its football team, and representing the school in track.

Our school only went to the 10th grade, as the government encouraged us to enter the work force. The headmaster of my school was Mr. Waters, a kindly man who recognized that my strengths lay elsewhere than the trades, he encouraged me to seek a position with the Commonwealth Bank of Australia. So at 16 years of age, still wet behind the ears, I became a full-time bank officer at the Richmond Branch. The Commonwealth bank was government owned with hundreds of branches all over the country. Richmond was a small 6 person branch, with a rather tyrannically 60 year old manager, who for whatever reasons, I seemed to rub him the wrong way. He delighted in making my junior status as painful as he could. It was bank policy at the time and we would consider Neanderthal today, that women could not be tellers, and that they had to resign from the bank on getting married.

After three years in Richmond I received a transfer to the larger more tolerable bank headquarters at Elizabeth St. in the city. This was a time when we posted all the savings and general banking entries by hand. A slow and laborious process, long since replaced by computers. However, it sharpened by number skills and even today I can add up long lists of numbers by sight. In those days the currency of Australia was in pounds, shillings and pence so you had three columns to add up. Fortunately, Australia changed over later, to a decimal system.

When I was 20 years old I decided to leave the bank and secured a position with the Commonwealth Government Department of Shipping and Transport located in the city. Then, at 22, I received a promotion to the Department of the Air Force located in Albert Park, hard by a large lake in a leafy suburb. With my foster father's serious illness, and attending a school that did not match my innate abilities, plus the usual adolescent struggles of finding oneself. Looking back it was something that set me off on a completely new path.

Some people think that these things just happen by chance, when an event or a person crosses our path for the first time. I am convinced it is by the grace of God. My saving grace happened in the 9th grade when the Reverend David Rettick, the personable, enthusiastic and insightful rector of St. Bartholomew's Burnley came to our school's religious education class. In Australian schools, clergy and qualified lay people are permitted to teach half an hour weekly religious education to students.

David had such a winsome personality, and a broad range of knowledge on many subjects that I and many others were drawn to him and what he taught about God's love.

It was not long before I became a member of the Anglican Church in Burnley. The first time I went to an evening service when I was fifteen, David asked me over to the rectory for a "cuppa" (tea) with his wife. I enjoyed myself so much that I did not get home until close to midnight, which worried my mother to no end. I found out later that she had called in person the next day at the vicarage to express her fear that I might turn into some sort of religious fanatic through the church's influence. I was really embarrassed. Neither she nor my father attended church, nor did almost all of my extended family. So they knew little about it.

I joined the church along with other young people and over the years I was in the youth group, and an acolyte, and a teacher in the Sunday school. David baptized me on my first Sunday at St. Bart's and a week later I was confirmed by Archbishop Booth at St. Matthias Richmond. It doesn't often happen that quick, and I had much to learn.

The church proved to be my anchor right through my adolescence. My grandmother had told me when I was 15 that I was adopted, but not to say anything to my parents as it would upset them, especially with my father so ill.

It was a very emotional time but as I said, the faith and the community of parishioners was a rock for me.

David was followed at St. Bart's by an incredible procession of gifted and faithful clergy whose influence on my life still remains today. Wilfred Holt, Geoff Sambell who became Archbishop of Perth, Lance Shilton and John Moroney who was a deeply spiritual and passionate priest. A war time chaplain in New Guinea, a bachelor who recently died in his 90th year.

Perhaps the one with the greatest influence on me was Lyle McIntyre, who came to St. Bart's in 1949. A truly charismatic person who drew an amazing number of people to him from all classes and professions, especially the youth. He was High Church, very pastoral, 30 years old, single and his Vicarage had an open door where we young people would share breakfast with him and enjoy his great sense of humor. It was he who encouraged me and two other young men to pursue a calling to the priesthood. Lyle was later to move to a large parish in a country town, Horsham in northwestern Victoria. He died at a relatively young age, and was mourned by thousands at his funeral whose lives he had touched.

In 1956, my foster father died at Heidelberg Repatriation Hospital at age 58. He had been a good father although somewhat dour and had great difficulty displaying his emotion, he was uncomfortable even hugging. Perhaps it was a reflection of his Highland Scottish roots. I was 23 years of age at the time. Mavis my foster mother died of cancer in 1984. She had been a wonderful mother to me, treating me as her own child with love, kindness, generosity and nurture. Likewise, my grandmother Annie Walker had helped care for me until I was 3, treated me with all the love and kindness and consideration right up to her passing at 84 years. I suppose those who are close to us in our early years, parents, siblings, extended family, have the greatest part in our formation as human beings.

At 21, I purchased my first car, an Austin A 40 with a canvas top. I purchased it from a friend who was going on a mission to New Guinea and could not take it with him. I was always a good saver, even on low wages. (I started at the bank on 4 pounds a week), and I was the only one amongst my friends to own a car. My wanderlust increased even further on weekends, I would load up the car with my friends, and off we would go to scenic places in all parts of the Victorian bush.

My second car was an Australian built GMC Holden which I purchased from my Aunt Olive. It was bigger than the Austin and served me right through my 20's. I would use it to transport colleagues at the seminary to lectures off campus.

It was around 18 years of age I found myself more and more drawn to the ordained ministry while still working at the Commonwealth Bank. What was taking place in my mind is not easy to pinpoint. Undoubtedly my increasing involvement in the life of St. Bart's with its dynamic clergy was having its effect on me. Also, the bank and the civil service convinced my thinking that this was not where I wanted to spend the rest of my life. Discerning God's call is not always simple. I saw no vision and heard no voices, but felt in my heart and mind that the Anglican priesthood was to be my vocation in life. Perhaps an inner voice. The church in later times has what is called "discernment committees", a group of lay people in a parish which meets with the candidate over a period of a year to mutually discover whether this person's calling is to the ordained ministry or to something else. This along with meetings with the Bishop and others is a way we now accept this person's candidacy to the priesthood.

However, first I needed to get more educational qualifications. The technical school only took me to the 10th grade, so I enrolled in a night school, Taylor College. It took me 4 years of night school, where I went after the work day, to finally matriculate, which is the entry into university. The Archbishop then accepted me as a postulant and I signed up to go to Ridley Theological College. However, before I was due to go, doubts began to cross my mind.

I wondered ... Do I really have the skills to be a competent, faithful priest? The thought of standing before people and preaching scared me. Could I be an able teacher of the faith? Could I be a helpful counselor to those needing help? These and other thoughts concerned me. So I wrote to the Archbishop to say I would not be going to Ridley in the fall. Two years went by. During that time I felt more and more uncomfortable in my job. Was the Lord pushing me to reconsider?

Finally I prayed "Ok Lord, I trust you that you will provide all that is needed to serve you faithfully".

Clergy always have to battle stereotyping, by the media and society in general. Here I was an ordinary guy interested in sports, girls, movies, current affairs, just like my peers. One evening I took Joan to a dance, after I was ordained and we were still courting, and some of her work friends said to her "you mean he really went to a dance?"

So in 1956, at the age of 24, I entered Ridley College of the University of Melbourne. Ridley was founded by Evangelicals, a wing of the Anglican church. It provided the majority of the clergy for our diocese. It was a three year course of scriptures, doctrine, church history and pastoral studies, plus New Testament Greek. I spent more time on Greek, not an easy language with a Cyrillic alphabet. By the grace of God I graduated and with 8 others was ordained to the Diaconate in St. Paul's Cathedral in 1958 by Archbishop Frank Woods. In the Anglican tradition one serves a year as a deacon. A training and apprenticeship time.

While staying in seminary we were required to do field work. This was usually on a Sunday and one other day. For the first 2 years I went to All Saints Clayton under a dynamic, charismatic Vicar, Bert Neal. He had 3 churches, and later went on to found and become the first headmaster of Gippsland Grammar School in Sale. He was sadly to die young leaving a wife and 3 young girls.

In Clayton I assisted with Sunday services, led a youth group, and visited parishioners. In my 3rd year I went to St. Eanswythe's Altona, a small church, where as a seminarian I was virtually in charge, except when the vicar in a nearby church came to celebrate communion. I was learning a great deal about parish ministry and really loving it.

Ridley College only had 60 students including some studying for secular classes. I greatly enjoyed my seminary experience and forged some lifelong friendships including Brian McGowan, Ray Colyer, and Geoff Glassock, who was to be best man at my wedding. The principal of the college was Dr. Barton Babbage, a New Zealander who also served as Dean of St. Paul's Cathedral in Melbourne, and later was to become Dean of the Sydney Cathedral. Ridley lived on the edge financially . Our rooms were small and sparse, but comfortable enough. Meals were pretty basic, I am sure the cook did his best on his very limited budget. Because we had spaghetti so many nights, it became one of my least favorite foods. Weekends we could go home, and I would stoke up on my mother's finer fare to sustain me for the days ahead.

After my ordination to the diaconate in 1958, I was assigned, no choices allowed, to the parish of Emmanual Oakleigh, a bedroom suburb filled with young families. There were 300 children in the Sunday school. There were also two daughter churches in Clayton and Huntingdale. The Vicar was the Rev. Rich McCall, a hardworking, faithful priest from whom I learned much about parish ministry. There was no church housing for a Curate, so a call went out to the parishioners asking if anyone could board a young bachelor clergyman for two years. The Ulhorn's bravely said they would take me into their comfortable home. The Uhlhorns were older empty nesters, who sang in the choir. They treated me like a son, even spoiling me with nice meals, doing my laundry and other acts of kindness. At Emmanuel there was an attractive Sunday school teacher who worked at a large insurance company. She lived down the road from where I boarded. She loved sports, and was a good tennis, badminton and squash player. We were married in Emmanuel Church Oakleigh, on November 5, 1959 with her sister June as maid of honor and with Geoff Glassock, a clergy friend, as best man and childhood friend Tom Brown, as groomsman.

The antiquated rule of the insurance company at that time was that a woman had to resign when she got married.

For our honeymoon we decided that we would take two weeks and drive our car to Sydney, and then back along the beautiful New South Wales and Victorian coast road, a journey of around a thousand miles. Joan's father, Ken offered us the use of his trailer which hitches on to the rear of a car. He loved his trailer which he stayed in on weekend trips. We only got about a day and a half into our journey when our car blew a gasket and we became stranded in a lonely caravan park. This small town had no parts for us, so they had to send to the city while we waited. On our way at last, nearing Sydney we were going around a rotary and the trailer hitch came loose. The trailer began to sway dangerously, and it was also tearing up the pavement. Somehow I managed to pull over to the side to rehitch it. I couldn't even think how I would explain to Joan's father how I had badly damaged his beloved trailer. Not a good start to a marriage I thought. Luckily no real damage.

Joan's parents, Ken and Doris Looker, who were originally from England, were regulars at Emmanuel along with their other daughter June and her husband Bruce. Joan's brother, John, was living in England where he met his future wife Jean.

In 1959 I was ordained to the priesthood, Archbishop Woods again presiding in St. Paul's Cathedral, Melbourne, with many of my family and friends present.
After the death of my foster father Roy, I decided to make contact with my sister Valda, who lived with her husband Ron and young daughters Heather and Beverly in the upscale suburb of Burwood. Knocking on the front door, Valda greeted me by saying "Oh so finally you heard, come on in". I was happy to have found a sister I had always wanted, even if years later, having grown up as an only child. Tragically, Valda was to die of cancer at the age of forty-five, just one week before the wedding of her daughter Heather to Gary Padgham.

My brother Don was living in Brisbane, Queensland, with his wife Fay and their six lovely children, Bruce, Sandra, Suzanne, Robert, Penny and Paul. Don and I of course did not grow up as brothers together, but we tried to make up for it in later life. During my many journeys from the U.S. to Australia, I would always go to their homes in Manly or Tingalpa for up to a week. I was always welcomed by the entire family. Don and Fay would take me down to the spectacular "Gold Coast" with its beautiful beaches, or up to the Glasshouse Mountains, so named by Captain Cook, as they reminded him of his part of England. My niece Sue would arrange dinners at some of Brisbane's nicest restaurants.

In 1960, Archdeacon Harvey Brown, Vicar of Holy Trinity Surry Hills, an upscale suburb of Melbourne, asked that I be assigned to him as he was going on a sabbatical leave to England and needed someone to take charge of his parish along with a retired priest Rev. Fred Falconer. I'd first met the Archdeacon in Altona when he came to speak at our festival there. He must have remembered me, and so had followed up in this way. Joan and I moved into the vicarage there until the Vicar returned. On the Archdeacon's return from England we had to move out of the vicarage and find new accommodations in the parish. We were to move three times in twelve months, staying in the homes of parishioners. A gypsy life at the beginning of our wedded life together.

Next I received a letter from Bishop Geoff Sambell, Melbourne Dioceses Assistant Bishop, he was later to become Archbishop of Perth. He had been a mentor of mine throughout my teenage years. In it he asked if I would go to the church in Stratford in the country Diocese of Gippsland, while the Vicar was on a six month sabbatical. One does not easily say "no" to a Bishop. So we headed down to Stratford, after saying a fond farewell to our many friends at Holy Trinity.

Stratford is a small country town a couple of hundred miles east of Melbourne, on a river, of course, named Avon, after its more famous namesake. It is sheep and cattle country. Joan and I settled into the very old and isolated vicarage which looked like it could be haunted. A previous Bishop had died there, after collapsing in the church with a heart attack. The only furniture we had was a table, four chairs and a bed all donated by parishioners. Sparse living. However, the country folk were very warm and welcoming. There were also three other small churches under my care, scattered over miles of sheep country. Busy, but I thoroughly enjoyed country life.

During this time, we were thinking that instead of another curacy in Melbourne Diocese, it would be a good idea to get some overseas experience. Our first thought was England, then again why not try the United States. So I wrote to the Bishop in Florida. He wrote back and said "No, we already have a couple of Australians". Next I tried Chicago, no reply. This is not going to be easy, I thought. At this time, some good friends from Holy Trinity were in Boston. Bob Vines was a scientist with CSIRO, studying ways to prevent less water evaporation, important in a dry continent like Australia. Bob's wife, Vera offered to go and see the Bishop in Boston to see if any parish there would be willing to take me. She must have been very persuasive, for one night at 2 a.m. we received a telephone call from Brockton, Massachusetts.

The Rector had incorrectly worked out the time difference between Boston and us. He invited us to come to his church in July as an Assistant Curate. Before we could go I had to get the permission of the Archbishop. The church was very strict with its clergy back then. We even had to get permission to marry, before two years after ordination  A clergy friend of mine who wanted to get married to his fiancé told the Archbishop he had to get married for "health reasons". He never explained what the "health reasons" were, but the Archbishop grudgingly gave him permission. Needless to say we were greatly excited. It was a step in faith for the Rector as well as for us. Usually you have to interview for a position before you are offered it but he did it sight unseen. In June we said our farewells to our family and friends who saw us off at Spencer St. station on our train journey to Sydney some 600 miles away. We reached the Victorian border at midnight and there we had to get out with our bags and catch the Sydney train to the other side of the border. The reason being, that the two states of Victoria and New South Wales, because of their rivalry, had built their railroads at different gauges so it was impossible to travel straight through.  Fortunately this has since been corrected. In Sydney we caught the P & O passenger line "Oriana", which made stops in New Zealand, Fiji and Hawaii before we disembarked in Vancouver, Canada.  After looking around that very beautiful city we caught the Canadian Pacific train, because we intended to go right across the continent by train. We first alighted in Banff, a most beautiful place, where we took a bus tour to the nearby glacier at Lake

Louise. Then reboarding the train we made stops at Calgary and Chicago before staying with friends in Buffalo. We finally arrived in Boston and were picked up by our Aussie friends, the Vines, and taken to their home in Belmont. We heard that the Rector in Brockton was getting anxious for our arrival as he was planning to go on vacation. The Vines, after a few days, dropped us off in Brockton where the Rector Dan Davis and his wife Lovis were awaiting us with dinner. We were taken to a second floor apartment on Silver Road which was to be our new home. Parishioners had completely furnished it down to a TV and pins in the pincushion. As we could only carry three suitcases with us from Australia, this was greatly appreciated by us.

My next project was to purchase a car and we decided on a second hand beige Volkswagen Beetle. Our grand adventure continued and now we were to meet the parishioners. Brockton was once the shoe capital of America, but had now fallen on hard times. A city of 90,000 people, it had neighborhoods of beautiful homes and then other parts which were gritty and dilapidated. The Church of St. Paul's was a beautiful stone gothic building with lovely stained glass windows and seating for 600. Attendance on Sunday was 400-500 with over 300 children in the church school. The members were an interesting mix of professionals and blue collar workers, a good number with English and Canadian roots. We were warmly welcomed and received many invitations for dinner. The Rector Dan Davis was a bluff navy veteran, very gregarious and generous, who also had difficulty at times in understanding my Aussie accent.

At my first wedding in the U.S., the rector had gone on his longed for vacation. In my very Aussie accent, I asked the groom in the service "Do you take this woman to be your lawfully wedded wife" I asked? He looked puzzled and said to me "would you please repeat the question?" He understood the next time.

In my new position, I assisted with the Sunday and weekday services, calling on parishioners, leading study groups and running a good size senior high youth group.

We decided that we would take the youth group to New York City, a distance of nearly 200 miles for three days. There had to be a lot of planning to take 18 young people with 6 chaperones on such a trip. Many of them, like us, had never been to New York so we were all very excited. Six carloads of us set off early on Friday morning. I had planned a whirlwind tour for them, including The Empire State Building, Radio City Rockettes, United Nations, Lincoln Center, Macy's, and at night, tickets for The Barnum and Bailey Circus. They also had a few free hours. Some of the boys took a taxi, and with little experience, didn't tip the driver who farewelled them with a few choice words.

On Sunday we attended the huge Cathedral of St John the Divine. I believe it's the largest gothic cathedral in the world. It is said that the aisle is so long that brides arrive at the altar out of breath. To my relief everyone arrived back home safely. In the youth group were two sisters, Valerie and Donna Kindberg, who have continued a valued friendship to this day, and visited me in England when I was serving in Swindon. Likewise Jack and Ruth Bates, from St. Paul's, who visited us in England.

Joan and I were excited to be in America, neither of us having been overseas before. We were determined to make the most of the two years we had planned to be there. On our first New Years Eve, we decided on the spur of the moment to drive our VW Beetle the nearly 300 mile journey to New York City to watch the famous ball drop at midnight in Times Square. So we set off with scant knowledge of the geographical layout of New York. Needless to say, we got lost, only to arrive at Times Square at 12:15 a.m. Just fifteen minutes after the ball had dropped, many people had left.

On our first vacation we decided to drive our little beige beetle to Florida, a distance of 1200 miles. As a Civil War buff I wanted to see the battlefields of Gettysburg, Petersburg, Harper's Ferry, Richmond and so on, as well as other scenic places. I think it took us a whole week before we even reached Florida. Gas was very cheap, under a dollar a gallon, and with the Beetles good mileage our travel costs were very low.

Sadly, St. Paul's was to close in 2005 due to lack of attendance and also falling finances and was sold to another denomination.

Our two years in Brockton was drawing to a close, and we were to return to Australia. However, in May of 1963, a search committee showed up at Sunday services, at St. Paul's. I was interviewed by Harold Dutton, the Senior Warden and Bobbi Hall. I guess they must have felt that I would be a good fit to be Rector of their Parish of St. Luke's in Scituate. For soon after, I received a call inviting me to be their Rector.

Rector, Dan Davis had arranged for us to have green cards which entitled us to stay in the U.S. as long as we wished. We had not asked him to do this but now his foresight proved invaluable.

As I was still a priest in the Diocese of Melbourne, I would have to be accepted into the Episcopal Diocese of Massachusetts. Before that could happen I had to take a psychological assessment. The psychologist gave me the Rorschak test, where you have to tell what various inkblots mean on a paper. I said I saw koala bears, kangaroos and wombats. The psychologist threw up his hands and said "I have no idea how to interpret that! You pass!"

After a further interview with the Bishop Stokes at which I confused the Puritans with the Pilgrims, I was accepted as a priest in the Episcopal church, part of the world wide Anglican Communion. We had come to love the people of St. Paul's, who had welcomed us as family. We were sad to leave them, but were excited to look forward to the first church I would be Rector.

Robert Edson, a seminarian who came to St. Paul's after I had left, later became the Rector at St. John's Hingham, and has become a life-long friend.

So in the summer of 1963, Joan and I moved into the Scituate rectory on Branch Street. Shortly after, I was instituted as Rector of St. Luke's, succeeding the first rector, David Smith who had moved to New York State.

Little did I envision then that I would be their Rector for all of 39 years. God moves in mysterious ways. It was to be here that our three children were to be born at South Shore Hospital. Janine in 1966, Christopher in 1968, and Carolyn in 1971. They were to go through the entire Scituate school system, each graduating from Scituate High School.

Janine went to William Smith College in upstate New York, Christopher to Hartwick also in New York state and Carolyn to Western Maryland College. After graduation they all found good jobs. Janine becoming a Senior Vice President with Bank of America, Chris with TIAA CREF and Carolyn as President of McDermott Ventures.

When we arrived at St Luke's they had a church building. But no hall, Sunday School rooms, rector's office, parlor, parking lot or pipe organ. The Sunday School met in the Masonic Temple, where 100 children of all ages crammed into the basement. We mockingly called it the "Black hole of Calcutta". We also had a large debt on the church. Over a period of time we built Dutton Hall under the leadership of Senior Warden, Harold Dutton. It was in 1965 that we added the Gordon wing which consisted of an office for the Rector, a meeting room, and a comfortable parlor. Mary and Elizabeth Gordon, twin sisters of the president of Kidder Peabody paid for most of it. They did everything together, maiden ladies, great benefactors of St. Luke's, whose antics led us to chuckle often. On one occasion Joan and I were at their Scituate home for tea (they wintered on Beacon Hill in Boston) when I asked them if they had read a certain book. Elizabeth said to Mary, "Did we read it?" "Yes we did" said Mary. "Did we like it?" said Elizabeth. "Yes we liked it" replied Mary.

In 1973 the Gordon sisters provided the funds for a hundred car parking lot which was dedicated by Bishop Arnold. When the Bishop's radiator sprang a leak in the lot, someone quipped that the lot had been baptized as well.

The church is not just buildings, and we were growing to nearly 300 families, with 150 children in the Sunday school. The vestry and parishioners were committed to growth. As a bedroom suburb we had many people who were mid-level executives in their corporations and businesses, who after 4 or 5 years would be transferred elsewhere, often we would lose 12-16 families a year. Working hard we would get a similar number of newcomers into our fellowship. This was one of the reasons I felt a long-term ministry would help provide stability to a changing church community. As well, our family grew along with the parishioners families. It was also a joy over the years to baptize children, and then their children. The little "squeakers" whom I had baptized in their infancy, and later to have celebrated their marriage.

Our Christian education program for children and adults was ably directed over the years by Betty Dayton, Marge Williams, Kay Litten and Vivienne Leonard. St. Luke's has been blessed by the service of many fine music directors and organists over its history. Bill Adams and Kitty Duvernois performed musical miracles on an old, wheezy instrument on the back balcony.

A vacancy was then filled by Nancy and Ralph Farris. What a blessing. Nancy was a first class musician who treated us to the glorious music every Sunday. That made our spirits soar, and our worship deeply spiritual. Her husband Ralph had a long career singing with top tier choirs, and with his fine voice enhanced our worship services each week. Ralph produced and directed "Noah's Flood" which involved scores of our children and adults, and packed our church for two performances. We were saddened when they moved to New Hampshire, but we wished them well in their new home. Some years later we were to participate in a very moving outdoor service at their lakeside home for Ralph. Jean Collier who has a doctorate in music, has since increased the choir, while Debbie Carleton for many years has directed hundreds of children and adolescents, in enlivening our worship.

Over a long ministry you often become the towns unofficial chaplain. Offering the invocation to Town Meeting, at the dedication of the Town Library, prayers at the High School Graduation, blessing the boats in the harbor, prayers on Veteran's Day, Fourth of July and serving on the search for a new police chief, to name a few.

I was anxious for St. Luke's to be of service to the community and beyond. So, I along with others founded the Scituate church food pantry whereby anyone needy could come to one of the churches, later the Masonic Temple, to receive bags of groceries, and food vouchers to help tide them over. Laypeople from most of the churches willingly staffed the pantry, and still do today.

We also began a consignment shop in the church hall ably led by Barbara Swan, who along with faithful assistants, for many years provided nice clean clothing and an amazing array of knick-knacks to the community.

As soon as Dutton hall was finished, with the aid of Bobbi Hall and under the leadership of Pauline Jillson, we set up a nursery school for the town.

Our laypeople went every second Sunday to Driftway Nursing Home to conduct services for the residents. The High School baccalaureate service for the graduating seniors had fallen into abeyance. So we revived it and made it into an interfaith service. It was voluntary but a significant number of the graduates would come wearing their cap and gown, accompanied by their parents. When the public schools closed early on a Tuesday for teacher training, the churches provided a religious education program for up to 200 children. In the summer we also sponsored an ecumenical vacation bible school for town children. St. Luke's also opened its facilities to Alcoholics Anonymous, Boy Scouts, gymnastics and other charitable and service groups. St. Luke's annual fair was a favorite of the people of Scituate. It was held every November and people would line up at the door waiting to get in at 10:00 a.m. The parishioners worked hard for many months making and collecting items for sale. Their cranberry shortcake for lunch became a town favorite. Cheryl O'Grady has filled over 150 baskets each year for many years. In the five hours the fair was open, they made a profit of at least $17,000. I jokingly told them that even Filenes doesn't make that much in five hours.

Over the years it has been gratifying for me to see so many of our young people to go on to have successful careers. They have kept in touch and often brought a child with them to be baptized, prepared for Confirmation, Ted Leclair is one, who has gone on to be a Rear Admiral in the U.S. Navy Reserve. He kindly invited me to give the invocation at Fort Worth, Texas when he was installed there, something I greatly enjoyed.

I give thanks to all those members who willingly volunteered their time to put their faith to work in God's service.

Another fun group we started was a drama group, when John Rice produced several plays, English comedies, but some more serious, such as "Murder in the Cathedral". The casts were all enthusiastic parishioners.

I began to write a monthly column along with other clergy in the Scituate Mariner touching on religious and current issues, in order to reach a broader audience, who were not church attendees.

Jim and Alice Beal, on the tragic death or their young daughter Laura, established a Memorial Garden in her honor. This sacred space beside the church has been lovingly cared for and used by parishioners as the last resting place of their loved ones.

In order to deepen our spiritual faith we began a 12 week "Alpha" course. Alpha begins with a communal meal, followed by a video on a Christian topic, then we would break up into small groups to discuss what we had seen. Many reported that this experience had deepened their faith. One attendee, Jennifer Ronan along with her husband Matt Durant, was later to offer herself as a candidate to the priesthood. She had contracted ALS just before her ordination, and was assigned to a parish in Virginia, where after a four year battle she went to be with the Lord. Her courageous and faithful life is told in her autobiography "Sparrow", which has been used as a study in Marshfield churches.

One morning a young woman with her two young children showed up at our church office and asked if she and her husband and family could join St. Luke's, and I was happy to welcome them. Some years later Colette Wood felt a call to the priesthood. She studied at the Episcopal Divinity School in Cambridge, after a discernment committee encouraged her to apply. After ordination she served in Cohasset and has since become a much loved Rector of All Saints Whitman, as well as ministering spiritually to people with dementia. She has since moved to Virginia to be chaplain of a large Episcopal retirement community.

## ROTARY

A move was made in the town to form a branch of Rotary International and I was asked if I would care to join with others in becoming a founding member. Around twenty of us from all parts of the community held our first meeting at Pier 44 Restaurant. We decided to meet for dinner on Wednesday evenings. Rotary does a lot of good works all over the world as well as in its local community. Chiefly made up of business people, men only, since changed to include women, it requires your attendance every week, and to serve on one of its work committees. I jokingly said this is more demanding than church. There was lots of fun, camaraderie and fellowship in our various projects. Due to work overload I had to resign after 10 years.

In 1993 the Scituate Chamber of Commerce nominated me to be "Citizen of the Year". It was something that I had not expected but they explained that it was for my services to the Scituate community. I pointed out that I was not yet an American citizen, so a better title for me would be "Alien of the Year". The award ceremony was held at the historic Barker Tavern, before a crowd of the townspeople. Alden Mitchell, who was recovering from a hospital stay, was M.C. and present were the State Senator, Representatives and the Board of Selectman. Janine, home from college spoke quite movingly, and our church choir sang me an amusing ditty and "Waltzing Matilda". The 200 guests present entered into all the fun. After many speeches from people I had worked with, including clergy of other denominations, my response speech expressed my gratitude. I was so moved it was not easy to respond.

## FURTHER EDUCATION

Education has always been very important to me, especially after having to do four years of night school to get into seminary in Australia. On moving to the U.S. in 1961, I was determined to do further studies part-time, as my parish duties permitted. I enrolled at Eastern Nazarene College in Wollaston, a small well regarded liberal arts college operated by the Nazarene Church.

The chapel was compulsory. However, because I was taking care of St. Lukes, I had to often miss chapel. For this I was fined $5 much to the amusement of St. Lukes' parishioners who heard about it. After obtaining a Bachelor of Arts, I next took graduate courses at Boston State College and after four years I was awarded a Master's degree in Education.

Often my parishioners would come to see me as their pastor for marriage counseling and for work, family and personal problems. At that time there were few counseling resources on the South Shore. Feeling the need for more training in these areas and not wanting to give unhelpful guidance to those who sought me out, I went back to Eastern Nazarene College part-time, and obtained a Master's degree in Family Counseling. I now felt better equipped to deal with these situations in a positive way but still made referrals to those with more clinical experience and time.

## YOUTH WORK AT ST. LUKE'S

Almost every year as part of their confirmation preparation, I would take the class away for a weekend retreat. Many times it was to Briarwood a picturesque mansion on the coast of Buzzards Bay. After the diocese sold it we would then go to Bertram House in Duxbury owned by the Sisters of St. Margaret, an Episcopal religious order.

It required a lot of preparation for this retreat as keeping often twenty or thirty, 8th and 9th graders busy over a weekend needed careful planning. We would have a mix of study, film, worship and recreation. I was heartened to hear some of the young people telling me that they wished they could do it again the following weekend. Keeping adolescent boys and girls in their rooms after lights out kept the chaperones and me on high alert.

One memorable incident took place at Briarwood when the boys were all bunked together in one large bedroom. They had gotten hold of the foam fire extinguishers and proceeded to playfully spread foam all over the room including their beds in one unholy mess. The high school chaperone who was with them, to maintain order, gleefully joined in the prank, as well as our own son, Christopher. For this incident, we were barred from Briarwood for 2 years and had to pay restitution for the damages.

The vestry would each year go on an overnight retreat to Briarwood on Cape Cod. We found that getting away in a quiet environment, resulted in fresh ideas to use on our return.

For over twenty years with the help of Diane Sullivan, Cheryl Bordne, my family members and parishioners I organized semi-formal dances for 6th - 8th graders. At each dance virtually the whole class of nearly two hundred students showed up. We had a dress code, shirt and tie for the boys, and a nice dress for the girls. I am sure this meant for better behavior at the dances which elsewhere had problems. We were expected to have the standard police officer present, something I secretly deplored, for middle school students. The dances meant that all these students and their parents were aware of the presence of St. Luke's in Scituate even though they mostly had other religious affiliations.

Our St. Luke's youth group was not large in number as it was difficult to compete with the many programs offered by the schools and the Recreation Department. However, we did try to offer them something different, within faith based programs. On one occasion we took them to Boston Common on a Sunday where St. Paul's Cathedral held a service for homeless people and provided them a brown bag lunch. It was an eye-opener for our kids who had never before encountered a homeless person. We had quite a lot of dedicated parishioners who faithfully led the Youth Group over the years, including the Bates and Bob Montague.

The Roman Catholic religious order, SVD, was holding retreats for high school students on the South Shore in their retreat house in Duxbury. Father Ken Reed invited me to be part of the leadership team of the 3 day retreat which was modeled on the highly successful adult "Cursillo" Retreats and called the "Teens Encounter Christ". I participated in several and was impressed at the positive effect it had on these young people. Led by a fine priest and supported by a team of clergy, nuns and laypeople, it was non-stop for those three days, but a joy to see how the young people responded to the gospel message.

My confirmation class for 9th graders would run on a Sunday evening for 18 weeks, plus the Retreat. I tried my best to give these bright young people a grounding in the Christian faith. Towards the end of their preparation they, and their parents contracted for them to sign up to be an acolyte or to help in the church school or nursing home or another service project of their choosing. The majority signed up to be acolytes, and they were rostered to do two services a month. I was impressed as to their faithfulness over the 4 years they served. We never had less than 18 acolytes on our roster. True to the saying that "the kid holds the candle, and the candle holds the kid". As each class graduated to go on to college they were replaced by a new group. I still, many years later, get invited to participate in the weddings and baptisms of these fine young people.

After the church decided that all baptized people could receive Communion regardless of age, I decided to institute the practice of First Communion, feeling that reception of communion required understanding the meaning of the sacrament, and how to prepare to receive it. We decided to start with second graders. These children and their parents met for four weeks where together we explored our Christian faith and particularly Communion at an age appropriate level. It was something that I enjoyed immensely, culminating in these earnest little 8 year olds kneeling at the altar rails with hands stretched to receive the consecrated bread and wine.

Family events were also important in the life of our church. Each year family dinners were held in Dutton Hall on St. Luke's Day, a Passover Seder, on Maundy Thursday, Stewardship dinners at local restaurants and various other "chow" events.

Over the years several seminarians from the Episcopal Divinity school would be sent to us for parish training. One, Ernest Cockrell and his wife Jill became very good friends, and he also became a very effective Rector in Marion and California, where he shared with me a concern for justice for the Palestinians after several visits to the Holy Land.

One Sunday we rented a bus to go us to Boston and then set our families loose to explore whatever they wished in this historical city. At 4 p.m. we met at Old North Church, where a lantern was displayed in 1776 on the spire, to warn the people that the British regular troops were heading towards Lexington. Old North is a lovely house of worship, with pews with doors, and an attractive interior. I had the privilege of leading the worship at the 4 p.m. service, with our choir singing every song and I delivered a brief homily. It was a nice worship experience, and connected our families to their early history.

## DUAL CITIZENS

We had always wanted to take out American Citizenship, after we decided to live here permanently, however Australia would not permit dual citizenship at the time. We found it hard to give up our Australian citizenship so we waited. Eventually Australia changed its mind, having been pressured by its businessmen, and allowed dual citizenship. We immediately applied, and after being tested on our ability to speak English (the Australian variety was approved), and other civic matters regarding the U.S. Constitution we passed. At a ceremony in Faneuil Hall we obtained our papers. We felt very good as America has been very good to us.

## WEDDINGS

Most of my weddings went off without any serious hitches except for one bride who needed a glass of water to keep from fainting and a best man who fell over at the altar rails and had to be assisted out.

One wedding especially memorable was when a bride to be asked me if her grandfather could give her away as her father had died. I readily agreed. Grandad was quite elderly and hard of hearing. I told him at the rehearsal when I say "who presents this woman to be married to this man?", in a loud voice he would say, "her mother and I do". He agreed he could manage that. At the wedding I began with the words of the wedding service. "If anyone knows any reason why these two persons should not be joined in holy matrimony speak now". Dear old grandad in a loud voice proclaimed "her mother and I do". I don't know who was more startled, the bride or me. After a pause, I resumed the service and when it came to answer the proper question, grandad said nothing. He had done his part he thought.

We almost always had the Eucharist as part of the service. The bride and groom and I felt what better way to begin their married life together then sharing in the sacrament. All the brides looked beautiful on their wedding day. One bride wore a white micro mini skirt,

in the 1970's, and when she knelt for the prayer you could hear the congregation sucking in their breath. I wondered how their children would view their parents wedding photos 30 years from now.

I used to attend every wedding reception after the ceremony. After one service I arrived late at the restaurant where the reception was being held. They were eating lobster, which I joined in doing. I asked the guest sitting next to me "How did she know Denise the bride?" The guest replied, "The brides name is Angela." I had come to the wrong reception, my bride was in the next room. I hastily left my lobster, and went over to the other room, for their chicken dinner.

## JOAN AND THE AIRLINES

In 1979, a friend Peg Lee, suggested to Joan that she apply for a job with Eastern Airlines. Along with interesting work, it would mean that we would get discounted fares to Australia, and elsewhere. Her first position was with telephone reservations. In 1985 she was offered a job at Logan Airport on the night shift in the baggage department. Later she moved up to a ticket agent. Her hours were 5:00 a.m. to 2:00 p.m. On the winter days when it was snowy, she would get up at 2:00 a.m. in order to get to the airport on time. One snowy icy day her car slid off the road and she was taken to the hospital with thankfully minor injuries. When Eastern Airlines went out of business over an acrimonious labor dispute, she briefly joined Trump Air, the billionaire New York moguls venture and now President of the United States. Joan then joined U.S. Airways, when he sold it off, where she worked weekend and morning shifts. After working at the gates, she was promoted to supervisor. Finally she worked at the U.S. Airlines Executive Club for her last four years before retiring in 2005. Joan made many friends at the airlines with whom she remains in contact to this day. U.S. Airways was later to merge with American Airlines.

## THE SOVIETS COME TO SCITUATE

It concerned me and others that in the bitter Cold War atmosphere of the time many were demonizing the Russian people, and probably they us. The threat of a nuclear war hung over all of our heads. Was there any way to help defuse this disastrous situation? As a very small step I felt that somehow we must show that the Russian people were humans like us with the same aspirations, hopes and concerns for their families. So, with the help of an international organization, I formed a committee of Scituate citizens to bring four Soviet citizens to Scituate for five days. We arranged a very busy schedule for them and also arranged for them to stay in homes in town. The next five days were a whirlwind of activity, as we had them speak at our high school and primary schools, to service organizations, town leaders, lunches and dinners. We did allow them some respite with a visit to the Museum of Fine Arts and the Wentworth School. They were excellent ambassadors and many friendships were formed. The local and Boston media gave us excellent coverage.

Some suspicious doubters whispered that our guests could be KGB (Soviet Secret Service) agents. We never had the slightest evidence of this. Our visitors, by their warmth and charm broke down many barriers and stereotypes to the people of Scituate. After a farewell dinner attended by some 200 people at St. Luke's we said our tearful goodbyes to our new friends. We had done our best in our small way to break down the dividing wall between us.

One humorous note, and there was much fun and laughter during the 5 days, occurred at the end when I received a phone call from a lady who was organizing a program for our visitors in California. She being their next stop of their American trip. She said that she did not want to emulate what we had done in Scituate from what they were planning in California. I asked her what they were planning?  She said, "attending a mud wrestling event,  a Jacuzzi party, a trip in a hot air balloon and a hot rod racing event"  I said to her "Madam none of those, this is New England!!"

The people of Scituate continued to speak well of this visit for many months, and a video of the highlights was shown at my Citizen of the Year award night.
Over our 39 years in Scituate we were able to welcome many Australian visitors into our home.  Doris and Ken Looker, Mavis Low, June, Ann and Jo Gardiner.  John and Jean Looker, Stephen Looker and Michael Read. Lorna and Ian Brown, The Manns, Vicki and Rob Gillespie, Geoff and Val Glassock, Robert and Julie Leighton, Sue Leighton, Heather and Gary Padgham, Archbishop Geoff Sambell, Dean and Mrs. Barton Babbage,  Dr. Leon Morris, the Vines, Aunt Dorothy, Archdeacon David Chambers, the Cooks and Kane and his friend, Joe.

Although we were half a world away from our extended family and friends we were always able to keep in touch with them.  Our many journeys back to Australia will be told elsewhere.

## ILLNESSES

As a child I seemed to pick up all kinds of illnesses, pneumonia, whooping cough, shingles, influenza even suspected psittacosis which left me abed far more times than I wished and which unsettled my parents social life. I still remember a young doctor making a house call (a rare occurrence today) who after examining me played a game of Chinese checkers with me before leaving. Probably a better medicine than any in a bottle. From my 20's on I was blessed with good health. Later I developed type 2 diabetes. However, I was diagnosed with prostate cancer in 2000 and underwent 39 radiation treatments. As I did not want any fuss made, I kept it completely to my family and myself and the parishioners never suspected. Perhaps not a wise decision, but the treatment never affected my work.

## HINGHAM HOUSE

In 1980 I bought a duplex in a development in the town of Hingham. The reason being that as we were living in the church owned rectory, although rent free, we were not building up any equity for our retirement. Housing prices were escalating . The church had bought the rectory on Branch Street for $28,000 in 1959. When we left in 2003 it was valued at $465,000.

I rented out both sides of the duplex, quite unprepared to be a landlord. Some tenants respected the property, others did not, and even failed to make their rental payments on time or, in one case not at all. I of course relied on their payments in order to make my mortgage payments. On one occasion while vacationing in Australia we got a call in the middle of the night from the partner of a tenant asking me to evict her partner as they were embroiled in an angry fight. I explained to her that as the lease was in her partners name only, I could not do that.

We were happy eventually to sell the place, and the proceeds did help us to purchase our retirement home in Marshfield.

## SAILING

Living close to Scituate Harbor and seeing so many of the towns people enjoying their time on the water, I decided to join them and purchased a boat. A parishioner had an 18 foot sailboat for sale, including a dinghy and most importantly a mooring in the harbor. Knowing nothing about sailing, a friend Sally Saglio, who had sailed all her life offered to show me the ropes. Joan would say I had a "How to Sail" book in one hand and the tiller in the other. I enjoyed many sunny days sailing around the harbor and into the ocean.

One event that ultimately led to the selling of the boat occurred one late fall afternoon. We had gone out into the ocean off Scituate, and it was beginning to get dark. We started to sail back into the harbor but now the wind and tide drove us out. I had no motor as a Coast Guard friend had told me a good sailor does not have a motor on a small sailing craft. Bad advice. It was now dusk and I said to my companion that the Coast Guard makes a dusk patrol. I found out later they had stopped the patrols the previous week. It became obvious we could not get back into the harbor. So we decided that we would have to beach on to one of the stony beaches farther down the coast. This we managed to do and struggled up the beach to call an anxious Joan at home.

The next morning at 5 a.m. I raced back to retrieve my boat only to see that the tide had carried it out to sea. I next raced around to the Coast Guard station, asking them to kindly rescue my boat. They agreed to after breakfast, and they did. The kids and I went on the cutter to return it. After this adventure I was persuaded to sell the boat, though I kept the valuable mooring. The buyer, after a series of mishaps, sold it, but kept the spare motor. It became a family joke that every time the boat was sold the seller would keep either the mooring, motor, dinghy or spare sails and the boat always went for the same price $1000.

When we moved to Marshfield after my stay in England I purchased an eighteen foot Sea Swirl, and rented a dock on the South River, a short trip to the spit and out into the Atlantic. Carolyn and Chris delighted in taking out friends to view the very scenic North River.

## PARISH EXCHANGES

Coming from another country to the U.S. and with a yen for travel, something that seems innate in Australians, Joan and I decided that an inexpensive way to see other parts of the country and the world was to exchange homes, churches and cars. Usually for a month in the summer. Clergy salaries are not large so in this way we would not wreck our budget.

Our first experience was to West Palm Beach, Florida where services were held in a storefront, while the parishioners were fund raising for a church building. It was August and the weather is very hot and humid. The rectory where we stayed had only one air conditioner which was in the main bedroom. Needless to say the kids and we spent the nights and other times there. Florida beaches are quite beautiful and despite the heat we spent many enjoyable times in the warm water. We also spent time exploring Florida, visiting Cape Canaveral and it's space museum, the Old St. Augustine, Miami and beautiful Fort Lauderdale and its canals.

On our return home we found a note from our exchange family suggesting that we do it again next year. I replied that next time we would like to do it in February, in the New England winter, and the warm Florida days. I never received a reply.

The next year we exchanged with the Rector of Saranac Lake in upstate New York, located in the beautiful

Adirondack Mountains. It was a small town set on a pretty lake. It had a quaint Swiss style church and a comfortable rectory. The Rector was an Englishman who had a huge library, covering all the walls of his study. Joan's parents joined us, and her father could not get over how the books went from the floor to the ceiling. He and Joan's friend Marge Herring and I drove up to Montreal Canada for the Montreal World Exposition, where nations of the world had booths showing off their nations culture and treasures. It was fairly close by from where we were staying so we were able to do it in a day. We also visited Lake Placid where the Winter Olympic Games were held as well as many other places in the vast Adirondack State Park, with its magnificent scenery of mountains, lakes and trees.

## KEN AND DORIS

Joan's parents, Ken and Doris Looker came to visit us in Scituate from Australia in 1970. They stayed with us for six months while they found work in the area before moving to Marshfield where they house sat for the owners who were on an extended vacation to Europe. They then had a job offer in Phoenix, Arizona with the Cathedral there. I drove them in their car the 2000 miles to Phoenix, a journey which took us five days. The temperature there was 120 degrees fahrenheit, being August. Ken loved the heat even while working outside the Cathedral as their gardener. Doris decidedly not. After a period there, they left for Darwin in Australia's Northern Territory to be with their daughter June, her husband Bruce and their four children Annie, David, Paul and Jo. It was equally hot and humid in Darwin which has two seasons, hot and wet and hot and dry. The Gardiner family were loving Darwin, and the children were winning a room full of medals and cups in the swimming meets and as lifeguards.

While they were in Darwin, the deadly Christmas Eve cyclone of 1974 struck and wiped out the entire city. The Looker's and the Gardiners spent the entire night hiding under beds and managed to survive the harrowing experience. Both of their homes were destroyed. We in the States could not get any news of their whereabouts, as all communications were lost. Finally, we heard after several days that they had safely made their way back to Melbourne, eventually buying a home in Upper Ferntree Gully, an outer suburb. The Lookers moved to Inverloch in Gippsland, a lovely country town some 70 miles east of Melbourne. Ken was to pass away there in 1992 aged 88. We all fondly remember him as a good husband, father and friend. Doris then came to stay with the Gardiners. She died in 2004 at age 94, much beloved by her family and friends.

Bruce Gardiner was to die of a heart attack in a sad surprise for us all, as he appeared so fit. Jean Looker, John's wife and mother of Lois, Stephen and Andrew was to pass away in Tasmania in 2016.

## DENVER

For our next adventure, we headed to Denver, Colorado. The five of us were warmly received by the parishioners of St. Luke's church in Denver in their very picturesque state. The Rector there went to Scituate, leaving us a very comfortable rectory, a late model car, an apartment in the Rocky Mountains for our use, as well as a power boat and a small plane which of course we did not use. Curious I inquired how he could afford all that on a clergy salary. I found out that he was a successful building contractor before entering the ministry!

We were able to explore the magnificent Rocky Mountains including the ski areas of Aspen and Vail. I was also taken to see the fine Air Force Chapel at the Air Force Academy in Colorado Springs. It is built in three tiers, one for the Protestants, one for the Roman Catholics and one for Judaism.

We have many photos of the wonderful scenery of the Rockies, and the very enjoyable time we spent there.

## BERMUDA

We next began to explore outside of the U.S.A. and arranged our next exchange on the island of Bermuda. Bermuda, a British colony is only a short 1-1/2 hour plane ride from Boston. It's azure seas, golden beaches, warm and hospitable people, both black and white make it a virtual paradise. Our home for the month was an

18th century Rectory located on a knoll overlooking "the smallest bridge in the world" in the county of Somerset. It was an ideal location, the ferry to Hamilton the capital, was just a few minutes away. The Rector had kindly signed his car over to me, as visitors are not permitted to own or rent cars. A wise move considering the narrow Bermuda roads. Tourists must use either taxis, buses or rent mopeds. The latter can be dangerous for tourists not used to riding on the left hand side of the streets. In order to use the Rector's car I had to obtain a Bermuda driver's license. It was the most rigorous test for driving I had ever undergone. I believe because they want to restrict the number of licenses issued. Somehow I passed this grueling task and when they asked me would I like a license for one year, five years or ten years I responded "give it to me for 10 years, I don't want to ever take this test again."

The church I served was directly on the coast, painted white with a colonial era feel inside to it. The parish churchyard was in front of the church, the graves above ground due to the heavy rains and on a small island, usually shared.

August in Bermuda is hot and humid but it did not stop us from enjoying the beaches and exploring the island from St. George's at one end to the Naval Station at the other. We were reluctant to leave this lovely place.

St. Winnow's Cornwall.

Lostwithiel Cornwall.

Through Road, Burwood, Melbourne Victoria. Ray Leighton Low born in this house March 25, 1931.

Childhood home Richmond Victoria Australia.

Emmanuel Church, Oakleigh Victoria Australia where we were married in 1959.

The interior of Emmanuel, Oakleigh Victoria Australia.

Anglican Church Stratford Victoria, Australia.

S. S. "Oriana". The ship that brought us to America.

St. Paul's Brockton, MA 1961.

Our first residence in U.S. Silver Road, Brockton, Mass.
1961-1963, 2nd floor.

St. Luke's Scituate, Mass. Where Ray was Rector for 39 years.

The Rectory. Branch Street, Scituate, Mass.

Ray with Joan at his retirement from St. Luke's Scituate, Mass.

Carolyn, Christopher and Janine.

Our grandson Charlie, Carolyn's son.

Our grandchildren Doug, Abby, Sam and Sarah.

Ray's 25th anniversary at St. Luke's, Scituate, Mass. Carolyn is crucifier.

Children's story in church.

Confirmation class, St. Luke's 1990.

St. Luke's, Scituate, Mass.

Ray's exchange of churches. St. James Church, Somerset, Bermuda.

Christ Church, Swindon, England.

Ray with the Vicar Simon Stevenette, Christmas Services.

Brother, Don Leighton, meeting after 21 years.

Retired to 5 Buttonwood Road, Marshfield, Mass.

# ENGLISH EXCHANGES

Emboldened by all our successful exchanges we began to look even further afield. I placed an advertisement in the English "Church Times" looking for someone who might be interested in our Massachusetts location. One reply came from the Vicar of Symondsbury in Dorset, who wrote to say he would be happy to arrange an exchange. So the five of us, Janine was 6, Chris 3 and Carolyn 1 in June 1972, set off on United Airlines on what was our first overseas exchange. We caught a train leaving Heathrow to Dorchester where we were met by the Vicar, Ben Knight who drove us to Symondsbury, 15 miles away. We were taken to this large old stone vicarage in the heart of the village.

The church was a 13th century gothic building, located nearby and inside was a list of all the Vicars going back to 1320 AD!

We were warmly received by the villagers. The Vicar and his wife showed us around the parish before their departure to Scituate. We were invited by the "Lord of the Manor" Sir John and Lady Colfox for dinner, later in the week to their splendid Georgian manor house. From working class Richmond, to the table in the Manor House made me chuckle.

There were two other churches in the parish, Chideock and Eype, for which I was to be responsible. I did not endear myself to the Chideock church people, oversleeping the 8 a.m. service, and then making a mad rush to find the congregation, very patiently sitting there waiting for the service to begin. I can't recall ever being late for a service before or since then.

While in Dorset we traveled extensively throughout England especially in the south east region, including Glastonbury, and as far as Land's End in Cornwall, the furthest point west in England. We visited many of the cathedrals, and historical sites as time permitted. Another successful exchange.

Still enamored by our English exchange we proceeded to make yet another one, this time in Wyken, just outside of Coventry. It was not a good beginning. The bachelor American assistant priest did not inform us about his cramped apartment which was totally unsuitable for Joan, myself and our 3 young children. The Vicar came to our rescue and arranged for us to stay in a more suitable house into which we settled nicely. Coventry was heavily bombed in the war and the Medieval Cathedral was destroyed. A new more modern Cathedral was built nearby, closely linked to the shell of the old Cathedral. We were quite moved to see a burnt cross with the words "Father Forgive" inside of what remained of the old Cathedral, and then the new modern Cathedral rising like a Phoenix from the ashes close by.

Again we traveled this time to the north, seeing the beautiful Lake District and then going on to Edinburgh,

Scotland. We also went down to London with our American friends Jack and Ruth Bates from Brockton.

The people of Wyken were especially gracious, and even gave us some nice gifts on our leaving. What started badly, ended beautifully.

We found out later that the priest we exchanged with was rather eccentric, riding a bicycle around Scituate in his cassock and annoying our parishioners in other ways as well.

Believe it or not we were to embark on our third England exchange in July 1974, this time with the Reverend John Carr, Vicar of Shiplake, near Henley-on-Thames in Oxfordshire. Janine was now 8, Chris 6 and Carolyn 3 years old.

The church of St. Peter and St. Paul was built around 1150 AD, built of flint stone, with an attractive interior. Alfred Lord Tennyson, the famous poet was married in the church in the 1800's.

Nearby Henley-on-Thames, is the site of the famous Henley Regatta, which had taken place on the Thames earlier in the summer. Sally Saglio a friend and parishioner of St. Luke's arrived to spend a week with us. We were all invited out for a river cruise on a highly polished, well preserved boat by a retired London solicitor living in Shiplake. The children were delighted as we went through the locks. Lovely riverside homes dotted the banks of the river. We also took Sally to London to see the sights, and to Winchester Cathedral for the remarkable "Sound and Light" program which dramatically told us the history of this ancient Cathedral. Sally wanted to go to Devon from where her ancestors came, so we decided to make an excursion of it. The six of us set off crammed into a very compact Austin 100, with Sally in the back with Janine and Chris and Joan was in front with Carolyn on her lap. To keep up our spirits we joined in singing English songs such as "There'll always be an England" "Men of Harlech" and "Jerusalem". The children all joined in with enthusiasm, even three year old Carolyn.

One night on the way we stopped at an Inn where the women and kids slept in one room while I slept in what was once a broom closet. A single bed and a tiny dresser were crammed in and I could barely turn around. They still charged £15 as it was high season. We could not find any records of Sally's family at Newton Abbot as the Registry was closed. At some of the Churches we visited we made brass rubbings of knights and ladies pictured on the plaques of their tombs.

One day a parishioner who was a member of Lord's Cricket Club (M.C.C.) invited us to watch a cricket test match between England and Pakistan. As Lord's is the very heart of the game of cricket I readily accepted. To those who are new to cricket, the Tests as they are called last for 6 hours each of four days with a break for lunch and tea. All very English. Like every Australian schoolboy, I had played cricket growing up, so I was familiar with the rules. During the course of the game I needed to go to the "loo", so I found my way there. We were in the members enclosure, when I stepped up to answer natures call, I found a plate glass window in front of me with a clear view of the match. Cricket fans do not want to miss a moment of the action on the field. Someone just might be "out", while they were gone. That is how seriously the English take their cricket.

In 1981, the Rev. John Gallop who had retired from Rector of St. John's in Hingham joined me as part-time associate Rector. John was to become a faithful, hard working, beloved colleague for the next 23 years. In all that time I cannot remember us having a cross word. We would share the services and the preaching. He would cover for me when I would go off for my yearly vacation. John was very high church and he would jokingly say on my return "I have taken down the photos of the Pope, and put away the rosary beads before you got back".

John was a scholar and widely read. His sermons were always memorable and relevant. He was still active, his mind sharp even in his early 80's when I retired. His wife Helen was a very fine watercolor artist. One of her creations graces our living room as they do in the home of others.

John and Helen enjoyed a wonderful retirement, traveling each year from their antique colonial home to Europe, but also off the beaten track to Tibet, Cambodia, Peru, the Trans-Siberian Railroad, India, Australia and the Pacific. In every country Helen took many beautiful photographs, which they made into slides. Sixty and more people showed up for their slide show in our parish hall completely rapt at what they saw, and accompanied by John's learned commentary on what was being depicted. An awesome lesson in history, geography, archeology and culture. Parishioners will always remember his sense of humor and his distinctive chuckle.

Beatrice Hurwitch was an ordained Deacon from the Dominican Republic who joined our staff in 1980. Her husband had been the U.S. Ambassador there before their retirement to Scituate. Eleanor Gowen had been the Principal of Scituate High School before moving with her husband Ray to Montana. While there she had been ordained to the Diaconate, and on returning to the South Shore, she also joined our staff. St. Luke's was growing with 150 children in the Sunday school, so these clergy were welcome to our work, both in and outside the church community. Our outreach included services and visitations to the nursing home and hospitals, assisting at the church pantry, involvement in Diocesan programs, Baccalaureate and school and town events.

## DEAN

In 1998 Bishop Shaw appointed me to be Dean of the South Shore, with pastoral oversight of the clergy of sixteen parishes. I did my best to keep in personal touch with each of them, as well as holding monthly meetings to share in their parish doings and to inform them of diocesan programs and offerings. We tried to breakdown some of the isolation that parish clergy can feel. I spearheaded a drive by the deanery to support the mission church of St. David's in Halifax. Every one of the Deanery parishes pledged to contribute to the $20,000 annual pledge for a period of 5 years which was matched by the Diocese. A simple but attractive church was built on donated land.

This would cover the salary of a priest and the operation of the church. Halifax was surrounded by four towns which had no Episcopal presence, and it was expected to show a major growth in population. A newly ordained and inexperienced priest was appointed as the first Vicar. Sadly it was a poor fit and there was little growth. Then part-time clergy and deacons followed with little change and in 2010 the Diocese closed and sold the church. I still believe that with better leadership and the continuing support of the Deanery and Diocese a vibrant church would have happened.

## THE HOLY LAND

During my first visit to the Holy Land I was disturbed by what I had sometimes witnessed or had heard. The long ongoing bitter conflict between Israelis and Palestinians has created much suffering on both sides. There are many books which I urge you to read about this conflict and its aftermath. Canon Naim Ateek, an Episcopal

Priest and Rabbi Michael Lerner have both written excellent books worth purchasing.

In them, they document how many Palestinians had lost their homes and were forced into refugee camps. Many checkpoints were set up where the Palestinian civilians would have to wait for long hours on end to get to work or visit their families. The wait was often deliberate and there were cases of people who were ill, dying, and expectant mothers having to deliver their baby at the checkpoint. Home demolitions and illegal possession of land are common. Israel "settlers" regularly burnt the ancient olive trees, destroying the olive crop. The Palestinians on their part would respond with bombing attacks on Israelis.

As a result a huge 18 foot wall has been built. Israel has every right to build a wall or anything else on its territory. The problem is they have built almost all of it on Palestinian land, cutting off families from each other, and separating them from their farmlands.

I have always had an innate sense of justice and sympathy for the underdog.

When another opportunity arose to go to the Holy Land again in 1988 I jumped at it. Eleanor Gowen was a Deacon at St. Luke's and she arranged a guided tour for 11 of us to travel there. We caught the Royal Jordanian Airlines flight to Amman in Jordan where we stayed at the comfortable Regency Hotel. Next day we were bused to Mt. Nebo where there is a 6th century church built in the summit, and from where we could see all the way to the Mt. of Olives and parts of the Dead Sea. The city of Amman was booming with construction sites everywhere. We than headed to the ancient city of Jurash which was built by the Romans in the 1st century. It's ruins are impressive. A temple to Diana is surrounded by 163 columns which sway in the wind. As well, there is a large forum, and a long street lined with Corinthian columns. The next morning we crossed the Allenby Bridge into Israel. Our bus then took us through the desert to Qumran where the Dead Sea scrolls were discovered by a shepherd boy in a cave. The ruins of the ancient ascetic community of the Essenes is also on display. From there we went to another ancient city, Jericho, mentioned in the Bible. It is an oasis of green, way below sea level surrounded by desert. Our next hotel stop was in Tiberius on the Sea of Galilee. We had a room with a view of the sea in a first class hotel. After breakfast we took a boat to cross to the other side, but in the middle of the lake we tied up to another boat and a Methodist Bishop conducted an inspiring service of scripture and hymn on this lake which Jesus had himself crossed many times and performed some of his miracles. We landed at the ruins of Capernaum, in which is located the ruined synagogue where Jesus had spoken. Further on we went to the Mount of Beatitudes the spot where Jesus delivered them.

We then journeyed on to Jerusalem, a city filled with biblical history. West Jerusalem is filled with apartments, offices and buses as bustling as any western city.

We had come to see the old city, situated behind high walls. Going through St. Stephen's gate we came to the Wailing Wall, all that is left of Solomon's temple, where many Jewish people stood swaying with their prayers and tucking written pages into crevasses in the wall. Close by is the Dome of the Rock with its golden dome, and the place where Muslims believe that Mohammad ascended into heaven and the place where Abraham almost sacrificed Isaac. Unfortunately it has been a flash point for riots, where Muslims and Jews have clashed.

We arose early the next day to go to the Church of the Holy Sepulcher, the place of Christ's crucifixion and resurrection, to hear Mass by a Polish priest who gave us communion. We also went to the Upper Room where by tradition, Jesus celebrated the Last Supper the night before his crucifixion.

We went to other biblical sites I had previously visited, except at the site of the Ascension where I had a brief camel ride.

We also visited Gordon's tomb, named after the British general who was killed in Khartoum. Gordon believed during a visit to Jerusalem that he had discovered the original place of the Crucifixion and Resurrection of our Lord. It certainly had an authentic look with a hilltop and a garden tomb. Most scholars reject his claim, but it has more of the atmosphere of the events than the traditional sites.

We crossed the Allenby Bridge into Jordan to catch the Royal Jordanian flight home. It had been an added pleasure to share our experiences with eleven parishioners who all greatly appreciated all that they had seen and heard.

It was time for us to leave, having had many experiences that we shall never forget, and which has made the events of the Bible very much alive and with new meaning for us.

## SEARCH

On my return I confided with an American Jewish friend, Dr. Ned Hanover, what I had found on my visits. His response was to challenge me with the words "Well what do you propose to do about it?" Ned had founded and headed up a small human rights organization called "Search for Justice and Equality in Palestine/Israel" "SEARCH" for short.

SEARCH's main work was with American newspapers and other media in trying to get them to give a greater balance in their reporting and stance on the conflict. At that time the media was heavily Pro-Israel and very much influenced by the Israeli lobby especially AIPAC. SEARCH pursued its mission by meeting with newspaper editors, holding forums and lectures, writing letters to the editor and participating in rallies and any way they could get our message across.

So I joined SEARCH and did all of the above, including appearing on the TV program "Greater Boston", speaking on the radio, sponsoring Diocesan resolutions, lobbying clergy and along with our Bishop Shaw picketed the Israeli Consulate in Boston. I invited several speakers to come to St. Luke's and share their experiences in the service and at the coffee hour. All this was done in the time I had after I had fulfilled my parish duties at St. Luke's. This became my outreach ministry.

I am typically a consensus builder and not confrontational, but my sense of justice, as an important part of my personal Christian faith, drew me to understand that only a two state solution in the Holy Land would bring about peace between Israelis and Palestinians.

The continuing expansion of Israeli settlements on the West Bank is counterproductive to peace and certainly not in Israel's long term interests. The Trump administration has also setback negotiations, by contrary to the U.N., and all our allies, given the recognition to all of Jerusalem to the Israeli government.

I like to think that SEARCH had in a small way helped to bring some balance to the media on this issue. Sadly, the political establishment remains in lockstep in support of the status quo. After many years of battling for equal justice, Ned contracted pancreatic cancer and passed away. In my eulogy at his service I said that I considered him to be in the same mould as that of the Biblical Old Testament prophets.

I had served for several years as the president of SEARCH alongside some very dedicated people. After Ned's death it was decided that we would pool our resources with a larger Californian human rights group with similar goals to SEARCH.

I later joined an organization "Jewish Voice for Peace" composed mostly of Jewish people, who are appalled at the treatment the Israeli government metes out to the Palestinian people who for nearly 50 years have been under harsh military occupation on the West Bank.

## THE HOLY LAND

I made a third visit to the Holy Land in 1998. I was briefly detained at the Tel Aviv Airport, I believe due to my work with "SEARCH" and questioned as to "Was I carrying any literature?" and "What was my purpose for being there?" Some young Palestinians were also being questioned, only more vigorously. My purpose was to visit some of the holy places again, and to meet with Palestinian Christians. I stayed at St. George's Pilgrim House which is close by the Old City. I went to visit Canon Naim Ateek an Anglican priest in the Diocese who had founded "Sabeel" an international organization working on justice for his Palestinian people. He told me how "The settlers" were destroying the ancient olive groves, harassing the farmers and taking their land and water as the soldiers stood by.

I decided to shift my accommodation to Christ Church Hostel at the Jaffa Gate, even closer to the old city. While there, I met a Roman Catholic priest who was on a pilgrimage and we struck up a friendship. It turned out he was soon to go to Jamaica to be consecrated as Bishop Dufour of Montego Bay. Several times over the years he would invite me to come visit, but sadly I never got around to it.

My third visit further convinced me that there had to be a Palestinian state alongside Israel if peace with justice was to come about.

## ZIMBABWE

In 1986 St. Luke's established a parish link with St. Mary's Harare in Zimbabwe. The goal being to give mutual support and fellowship within the Anglican Communion. I decided to make personal contact with the parishioners of St. Mary's, as well as to take along financial gifts for their work.
I took a flight from Boston via Frankfurt to Johannesburg in South Africa, some 18 hours, then a short flight to Harare. It so happened that the Rev. Louis Pitt from Massachusetts was the Acting Dean of the Harare Cathedral. He was away on vacation but he offered me to stay in the large and stately Deanery. During the 6

weeks I would be in Zimbabwe, I would eat many meals on a very long table and be waited on by a native Zimbabwean who prepared my meals and who lived in a small house with his family at the bottom of the garden. I felt embarrassed by this sort of colonial situation especially as I had grown up in an egalitarian Australian environment. At the time I left I supplemented his meager wage with a grateful remuneration.

The services at St. Mary's, our linked parish, were jam packed with the native Shona people. The singing was spectacular, most of the hymns being in Shona, which I did not understand but appreciated the enthusiasm. The parish was mostly run by three Anglican nuns who lived next to the church. As was customary, I blessed individually over 100 children at each service. I was very moved at each service.

The Anglican Cathedral in Harare is an impressive building, large and well kept. Sadly it was taken over by a maverick Bishop, who was allied to the tyrant Mugabe and the loyal clergy and many laity in the parishes as well, were forced to meet in the open air as their churches were confiscated. Since then, following a visit from the Archbishop of Canterbury, the maverick Bishop has been deposed and most of the churches reopened.

Wherever I went, the people were unfailingly hospitable inviting me for a meal with their family. A white Zimbabwean couple Jeni and Tim Webb, introduced to me by U.S. friends Guy and Sheelagh Wannop, even loaned me their Mercedes so that I could drive to the south to visit the "Great Zimbabwe Ruins", a very mysterious centuries old city of unknown origins. Coming back I encountered a roadblock manned by heavily armed native Zimbabwean soldiers. At that time they feared an invasion by white apartheid South Africa. I felt nervous, as I fumbled with the unfamiliar door lock. I must have looked harmless, for after questioning they allowed me to proceed. Later that week I visited a remote tobacco farm, the homestead being surrounded by high electric fences and with guard dogs as it was close to the border with Mozambique, where there was the ever present threat of armed guerillas raiding the farms. Nevertheless the farm family treated me with great hospitality. Almost all of these white farmers have been dispossessed by Mugabe without compensation, and the farm production has plummeted. The Webbs and other friends the Wannops have since fled to Australia.

Before my time to leave I first caught an old "Caravelle" jet to Victoria Falls. They are truly spectacular and breathtaking. Discovered by the missionary explorer David Livingstone whose statue stands near by. The volume of water going over the falls is overwhelming. I stayed over at the historic Victoria Falls Hotel, which is only a short distance from the Falls.

Finally I took another plane to Hwangi National Park in the north. I was thrilled to sight giraffe, rhino, two lions, zebra, ostrich a water hole. It was nearing the end of our safari trip in the camp's van and we had not spotted a single elephant. So I said to the native driver "I will give you five pounds if you can find an elephant". Twenty minutes later he found a dozen elephants at a waterhole. "Five pounds per elephant" he said. "No, no" I replied "Five pounds for one!" Finally he agreed. Phew.

I had wanted to visit South Africa being so close and applied for a visa. It was denied. I believe that clergy were under suspicion in apartheid South Africa as Archbishop Tutu and his clergy were most vocal in their opposition to this evil.

I fell in love with the land and people of Zimbabwe, and I hope strengthened the ties between St. Luke's and St. Mary's.

## SOUTH AFRICA

My second try to enter South Africa happened in 1995. The Rev. Richard Menees and his wife Martha invited me to come visit them in Valwaater in the Transvaal.

I had known them while they were serving in a South Shore parish, now they were serving in this rural Anglican parish. Their home was out in the hinterlands, with nary another house for miles around. I flew into Johannesburg and was to be picked up the next day. Wanting to explore the city, I was about to leave the hotel with my camera slung over my shoulder when the black woman hotel receptionist called out to me "you probably won't come back with that camera". I remembered then that Jo'burg as it was known had one of the worst crime rates in the world. The homes looked like fortresses with iron gates and barred windows. Needless to say I took her advice.

Richard picked me up the next day as he had promised. We drove for many hours to the north through dry country. Finally arriving at their home, I felt like I was in the Australian outback. After a meal, I was shown to a small one bedroom whitewashed "cottage" a distance from the main house. There were no locks on the door and nervously I wondered what wildlife might come calling or even two legged ones. Way out on the veldt it was incredibly quiet and yes peaceful even.

Richard and Martha were the souls of hospitality. On the Sunday I traveled with them to their quaint church and small congregation. This was Boer country and the Dutch reformed churches were huge.

The next day the three of us set out to visit the famed Krueger National Park by Land Rover. It was quite a distance away, east of us, but undeterred we stayed a night with their friends before reaching the park.

Kreuger National Park is probably the best known and most visited of parks in Southern Africa. Driving through it in our Land Rover, we were able to view close up herds of elephants, lions, zebra, rhinos and more. The park has many lodges and camping places located throughout the vast area.

After our return, Richard drove me to Soweto, a town of mostly shacks with many thousands living there under appalling conditions. The goal of the government is to narrow the gap between grinding poverty and luxury living. It will take a long time I thought as we drove around the town.

I had always wanted to visit Capetown in the south of the country, and here was my chance. Richard drove me the 2 hour trip to Jan Smuts Airport in Jo'burg where I caught a three hour flight to the Cape. If I had taken the train it would have taken me 26 ½ hours.

I rented a compact car at the airport to enable me to drive around the beautiful area. Capetown is surrounded by mountains, two oceans, the Atlantic and Southern with splendid beaches and tiny coves with attractive homes, built on cliffs overlooking the water. Here was somewhere I could easily settle down in. I took a cable car ride to the top of the iconic Table Mountain. It is flat on top just as its name tells us, with breathtaking views of the city, the oceans and surrounding countryside. All was quiet except for the sound of a light wind. Rabbits, tortoises and even deer live up there.

Next on my must see list was the famed Cape of Good Hope, the most southerly part of all Africa and where navigators "turned the corner" as they headed for India and the Indies. It did not disappoint. From there I drove along the Garden Coast road which stretches along the southern coastline of the nation. What a delight, mountains on one side, the ocean, bays and coves on the other. Green pastures with grazing sheep and cattle, wineries and vineyards would often insert themselves between the sea and mountains. Dutch style homesteads also dotted the landscape, testifying to their Boer heritage. I stayed at some very comfortable B&Bs along the way with their hospitable hosts.

With the Rand at 3.3 to the U.S. dollar it was an inexpensive stay. However at one B&B, I called some friends in Zimbabwe, and they charged me R300 for a 13 minute call. I shared my unhappiness with the proprietor and after some discussion reduced the charge to R150 which still worked out at US $45.
After returning my rental car, I flew back to Jo'burg where Richard met me for the long drive back to the well named "Rainbow's End". Richard and Martha not long after returned to California, their allotted time was over.

To get back home to Boston, I took a South African Airline flight that flew the length of all Africa and then to Frankfurt Germany where I was to take a flight to Boston on U.S. Air. Best laid plans of mice and men. The flight was full so I had to find a hotel for the night. Back the next morning, I thought that I was on, but they took me off the bus from the terminal to the plane on the tarmac. To make matters worse, they sent my suitcase on to Boston without me. I now had only the clothes I was wearing and one change of underwear in my carry on. I had to scramble to find a hotel for the second night. Back again the next morning tired and frustrated and seeing the agents putting more people on well past the departure time, I foolishly complained to the ticket agent that this was my third attempt to get on and that I had no spare clothes and the hotels were costing me over $150 a night.  This is all a "no no" for a pass rider.  The unsympathetic agent abruptly asked me "What is the employee number you have?"  I quickly apologized to her and practically ran out of the terminal.  When I told Joan later what had happened she was rightfully furious.  I could have lost all of our pass privileges.  You never complain.

Now I was stuck in Frankfurt for the fourth day, each night I stayed in a different hotel, each one cheaper than the last as I was fast running out of cash.  However, I decided if you can't beat them you join them.  Frankfurt is an attractive modern city, it was 75% destroyed in the war, but has since been rebuilt.  The American Army had a major base there and it was a financial hub of Germany.  A Gray Line bus took me to the quaint older part of the city with its brightly painted buildings and museums along with some raunchy establishments.  With more time on my hands I took the train to Mainz with its enormous ancient cathedral.  The Bishops in the middle ages had great power with a voice in electing the Holy Roman Emperor.  Denied boarding once again, I took the train to the beautiful university city of Heidelberg on the Rhine River, with its ancient ruined castle hovering over the city.

Crossing the ancient bridge over the Rhine gave me another perspective of the city from one of the benches where I rested and contemplated how many times over the centuries the Rhine had overflowed flooding and damaging the city.

The fifth morning I took the train to the airport, such is the drawback of pass riding. A ticket inspector asked for my ticket for inspection. He began to speak rapidly and angrily in German to me. I told him I did not understand German. He then said curtly "you have a child's ticket". Apparently I had mistakenly pushed the "kinder" child button on the ticket machine. He muttered something in German, I am sure not complimentary, and charged me the corrected amount without a fine. I was left embarrassed by the stares of the other passengers.

On arriving at the airport I discovered that Joan had come to my rescue, pleading to them to get me out of Frankfurt. I got the last seat of a flight to Pittsburgh, then Boston. You need to be flexible and patient as a pass rider, yet the benefits outweigh the inconveniences.

## RETIREMENT

On December 31, 2002, I retired after serving for over 39 years as the Rector of St. Luke's. It was the longest tenure of a Rector in the diocese for a long time. Even then it was difficult for me to leave the people and Town of Scituate whom I had grown to love.

I had been a Curate at St. Paul's Brockton under the Rector The Rev. Daniel Davis in 1963 when Harold

Dutton and Bobbi Hall called me to be the Rector at St. Luke's. I felt that together the parishioners and clergy had accomplished a lot over my tenure. It is not easy to measure exactly what effect the church had on the lives of the people of Scituate, however on my retirement I was presented with two volumes of letters, cards and photos that attested to how the church's ministry had an effect on their lives and how their faith and that of their families had deepened spiritually. They told how their active participation in the life of St. Luke's had given them a better understanding of how Christ was calling them to serve him in many different way. This was humbling and heartwarming to me and I keep those volumes in my bedroom bookcase. My long term (15 years) parish administrator, Pat Forsberg, who had been a reliable and faithful support, compiled a list of my sacramental and other services. I had baptized 808 infants and adults, conducted 355 weddings and officiated at 429 funerals.

I was to add to that number at Trinity in Copley Square, but especially in England with a considerable number of weddings and baptisms, but especially funerals. I had also counseled with many people over those 39 years, and of course I cannot divulge their problems, but did appreciate their trust in their church that they came willingly to share what was in their heart knowing that we cared and wanted to help. There were some tough times during that 39 years with the economy in trouble. With the unemployment rate so high we held a series of meeting in the Gordon Room to help those in attendance find new jobs. We gave them tips on looking and how to write a resume, interviewing skills and especially helping to keep their spirits up in a stressful time not only for them but also for their family. A half dozen people a month would come by the office seeking a food voucher usually $50 - $75 to be cashed in at a local supermarket, as well as food made available at the Ecumenical Food Pantry held then at Father Bradley's Foyer of Charity. I had seen a lot of clergy colleagues move on to other churches and it was a joy while I was chairman of the Ecumenical clergy group to join with them in many projects together.

In the years that I was at St. Luke's, there were tremendous changes in the church and in our culture. Women were now ordained to the priesthood. Barbara Harris was the first woman consecrated a Bishop in the Anglican Communion. Gay marriage was authorized. I married Chris Lee to Robert Van Glahn in a joyous ceremony in Connecticut.

A committee led by Cheryl O'Grady arranged first a farewell party at the Scituate Yacht Club attended by parishioners and members of the wider community. Then a celebration at the 10 a.m. service with the Sunday school children and the junior choir with all kinds of presentations including cute notes from each child. In the afternoon we had an afternoon tea at the Immerman home at which Bishop Shaw attended. The final service was at 7 p.m. with the Bishop presiding, included Episcopal clergy, friends and clergy from every other Scituate church including the Roman Catholic. In this ceremony I handed back the church keys to the wardens, a wombat to the head of the Sunday school, a gavel to the Ecumenical Clergy Association, and a cross to the new dean of the South Shore. Our whole family was called to the front of the altar and senior warden, Paul Jevne presented us with a most generous check. The 200 people in attendance then retired to Dutton Hall for refreshments and a lovely cake.

I couldn't believe how the press covered my retirement. There were photos and stories in the Boston Globe, Patriot Ledger, Scituate Mariner and The Diocesan media. I jokingly said "Where was the Wall Street Journal?"

As we had always lived in the church owned rectory on Branch Street, the dilemma facing most clergy is where do you live after retirement? We did think of that several years before our retirement date. We bought a 1963 three bedroom Cape Cod home in Marshfield on Buttonwood Road, a pleasant area known as Holly Hill. I jokingly said "That if I stand on the roof I can see the Atlantic Ocean". Being on a steep hill, you have to have an all wheel drive vehicle to get up it in the ice and snow. The house was only 15 minutes away from Scituate, so easy for our kids to visit.

As I was still working, we needed to obtain tenants to help pay the mortgage and taxes. One tenant was a disaster, the other fine. The first failed to pay her rent for six months and allowed the basement to flood ruining all of its contents. We finally had to get a court order to get her out. The laws in our state are very protective of the tenant. We would have had to put her furniture in storage at our expense. Fortunately her divorced Marine officer husband moved her stuff out. I felt sorry for him as all his Marine memorabilia had been ruined in the flooded basement. Our friends helped us to remove some fifty bags of ruined stuff from the basement.

## TRINITY BOSTON

As a new tenant was living in our home, we needed to find a new place to live. Almost as soon as I retired I was invited to be on the staff of the iconic Trinity Church in Copley Square, Boston. Trinity is an architectural masterpiece, Romanesque, recognized as one of the ten best buildings in the U.S. by the National Guild of Architects. Inside are magnificent stained glass windows, several by Tiffany.

Such was the appeal of Trinity's Christmas carol services that there was a line stretching right around Copley Square of people hoping to get a seat in the church. I was sent out to hand out candies to the waiting people. The weather was usually near freezing, so I think keeping warm was more on their mind. Trinity seats 1400 people, so sadly many had to be turned away.. For those who did get in they heard the most superb music, and a very moving liturgy.

Renowned Architect, Alan Richardson had been commissioned to design and build Trinity by the then Rector Phillips Brooks later to become Bishop of Massachusetts. He was also the author of the much loved carol "O Little Town of Bethlehem".

It was for me an eighteen month temporary assignment, there being four other clergy and forty lay persons who helped carry out the many ministries of Trinity. It was a large congregation, over two thousand parishioners with an annual budget of over $3 million. The Rector was Sam Lloyd who was recognized as one of the best preachers in the country. There were two magnificent choirs, you could almost "hear the angels sing" they were so spiritually transporting and uplifting. Services were held at 8 a.m., 9 a.m., 11:15 a.m. and 6 p.m. I was mainly rostered to celebrate at 8 a.m. and 6 p.m., and assist at the other two. I always greatly enjoyed the 6 p.m., which was mostly attended by young people who at the great thanksgiving part of the service would encircle the high altar.

Besides the services, as part-timer, I would take communion to patients in the hospital or home, give talks to the church school children, attend study groups and do pastoral counseling as asked. I was asked to mentor Bill Franklin who wanted to be ordained to the priesthood. He was later to become the Bishop of Western New York, so I guess I didn't do too bad a job. I was to make many delightful friends at Trinity with whom I still keep in touch. My time finished far too soon for me, I would miss the amazing music, the great preaching, the magnificent building and the hundreds of dedicated volunteers.

## WEDDINGS OF JANINE AND ROBERT AND CHRISTOPHER AND JANN

It has been my great pleasure and privilege to celebrate the weddings of my three children. Janine and Bob Beal were married at St. Luke's on in 1998. Following the wedding we had a fun filled reception at The Winsor House in Duxbury. When Sam arrived in 2003 and Sarah in 2006, I again had the privilege of baptizing them at St. Luke's.

Christopher and Jann Leonard celebrated their wedding in the Seaman's Chapel in Newport, Rhode Island also by me. Some years before, I had baptized Douglas and Abigail, children of Chris's first marriage to Betsy Brown.

## WEDDING OF CAROLYN AND MICHAEL

During my time at Trinity our youngest daughter Carolyn was married to Mike Spicer of Maryland. All was set for the ceremony at Trinity. Disaster. The Boston Red Sox had won the World Series of baseball for the first time since 1918 and of course there was a well deserved parade which was to draw over a million people that was scheduled that morning. The parade was to go right past Copley Square, the church's location, and the trolley driver who was to transport the guests said "There is no way we will be able to get to the church". I was watching the parade on TV and kept urging the "duck" drivers to keep it moving, as if they could hear me! In any case luckily it did go quicker than expected, and then would you believe it began raining, a real downpour, that quickly dispersed the huge crowd away from the church and the guests got to the church on time. This marriage was meant to be. The only hitch in the service was when the substitute organist played the wrong processional going down the aisle. I both did the father role and took their vows. At the reception at Rowe's Wharf I told Mike he has no excuses for forgetting an anniversary date. He, being a sports fan agreed. The reception was a joyous occasion and Carolyn made a beautiful bride and Mike a handsome groom.

During Joan's and my time at Trinity we rented firstly, an apartment in Brookline, from an Indian Hindu couple who were professors at Boston University. The pictures on the wall were of Hindu gods. When we invited friends for dinner they would jokingly suggest that we had converted to Hinduism. When this lease ran out, we rented another apartment on Broadway in Boston. I had always known that one day I would make it to Broadway! The owner was another Boston University Professor who was going on a sabbatical to England. We loved that 5th floor apartment which looked out on the surrounding rooftops and to us it looked like Paris. It also looked down upon a transvestite bar, which piqued my curiosity and kept me up late rubbernecking. The professor was looking to sell it but the price was far outside our range with the incredibly inflated Boston housing market, it must have at least quadrupled in price over the years. Joan appreciated how easier it had become for her to commute to her work as a supervisor at Logan Airport. I also had an easy walk to Trinity.

## SWINDON

I was still in good health and decided that I was too young to sit around in a rocking chair and began to think maybe the Lord can still use me.

So I placed an ad in the English "Church Times" stating "American priest looking to serve in an English parish, no stipend needed". I received only one reply. It was from the Vicar of Christ Church in Swindon in Wiltshire. It had turned out that Angela, the mother of the Rev. Simon Stevenette had read the ad and passed it on to her son. God works in mysterious ways. He wrote me and expressed an interest in my coming. Joan, her airline friends and I were shortly heading for a holiday on the Dalmatian Coast of Croatia, so I told Simon that I would fly back home after the holiday via England and meet him in Swindon for us to see if we were a good fit. I went by train a 1½ hour journey to Swindon from London. then by taxi to Christ Church. Swindon had once been the hub of the Great Western Railways. It was chosen by the famous engineer Ichabod Brunnell in 1850 to be where the locomotives and rolling stock would be built and repaired. It was estimated that 50% of

Swindon's workforce was at one time employed by Great Western. It has since all gone, except for an interesting museum with the artifacts and history of that time. Its present population is around 90,000. It has a mix of housing and some lovely parks and gardens.

Christ Church is a large gothic church built in the mid 1850's, not old by English standards, sitting on the highest hill in the town, it can be seen from all over the town. It can seat several hundred worshippers and it is said you can see the bullet marks on its spire which were fired by American airmen returning from their bombing raids in World War II.

The Vicar, Simon Stevenette and I hit it off immediately. In his late 40's, he was an energetic, innovative, cheery and sports minded cleric. He had an attractive, talented wife Nicola, and 5 polite, intelligent sons ranging in years from 5 to 16 years old.

In July of 2007 Joan and I traveled to Swindon in Wilshire to live in a three story brick dwelling owned by the church, which was also occupied by two young men on the 1st and 3rd floors with us in the middle. We were warmly welcomed by the people of Christ Church and its daughter church, St. Mary's. I was placed on the rota for Sunday and Wednesday services, as well as for weddings and funerals of which there were over one hundred a year. Most of them held at the local crematorium. Counseling, meetings and visitations to nursing homes and hospitals were part of my duties.

As I was a "house for duty" priest, I was supposed to work only 2 days a week plus Sundays which gave us time to travel on the off days. There was no stipend, but I did receive wedding and funeral fees.

We were inundated by the number of invitations to lunch and dinner by our gracious church members. We often accepted many invitations to the vicarage for a meal with the Stevenette family.

As Joan was committed to babysitting the grandchildren she would come back and forth across "the pond" when she could. I had purchased a small car for my parish duties, so I was able to take off for overnights on my days off. The beautiful Cotswolds were an hour away and I explored much of the area, including Bibury, Broadway, The Slaughters, Burton-on-the-Water and other beauty spots in this justly famous part of England with its thatched cottages and quaint villages. I also made a couple of visits to Lostwithiel and St. Winnows in Cornwall, home of my forbears who in the 1860's left for Australia. Attending a service at St. Winnow's where my ancestors were married was quite a moving experience. The church sits in a lovely rural hamlet by the river.

One week, I boldly set off for the far north of England, visiting the City of York with its really magnificent York Minister. I had to get to Canterbury Cathedral, the heart of the Anglican Communion, founded by Augustine in 630 A.D. and stayed at the comfortable guest house on the cathedral grounds. The cathedral is magnificent both inside and out. It contains the shrine of the martyr St. Thomas A'Beckett.

Driving back to Swindon on the road, I was rear ended by a driver on his cell phone, causing whiplash and a badly damaged car. I somehow managed to drive it back to Swindon where Ailsa Palmer and Verity Brookes insisted that I go to the hospital, where I was treated and released. My insurance company provided me with another car until I got my own.

I had lots of company while in Swindon and later in Corsham. Janine and Sam, Chris and Jann, Carolyn and Mike, Annie and Frances, Valerie and Donna all came to stay briefly. Sam was particularly enthralled with Lego land and the Dinosaurs in a London museum. His photo was even taken at a fair and was in the local paper!

Christ Church is a dynamic church, lots of outreach and innovation, ecumenical, being in partnership with the local Methodist and Reformed Churches. No less than five of its members have been ordained in Bristol Cathedral, plus it has several licensed readers. One outreach of note is called street pastors, where trained, volunteer laypeople go out on the streets of downtown Swindon on Friday and Saturday nights from 11 p.m. to 3 a.m. to be there for the hundreds of mainly young people, and to help in any way they are needed. Their work is appreciated by the police, for their presence has calmed many a situation. I did not participate as I found I couldn't keep awake at such a late hour.

Christ church has an excellent choir directed by Tim Eyles and they have been invited to sing in Salisbury, Gloucester and Bristol Cathedrals.

While at Christ Church I was called on to celebrate several weddings, a task I always found most enjoyable. The Church of England being the established church had a lot more paperwork and bureaucracy than the church in America. There was one lovely wedding that I celebrated, that during the service the bride and groom and the witnesses all came into the vestry to sign all the appropriate certificates which they nicely did. However, the following Monday, the clerk of the vestry told me that I had forgotten to have them sign one of the several documents. So the bride and groom had gone off on their honeymoon not legally married. I had to wait until they returned to get them and their witnesses back to church to complete their signings. I must admit that they were good sports about it. The parish clerk chided me not to let it happen again.

I also married a gypsy couple in a very elaborate and expensive wedding. The bride being 16 and the groom 17, something I had some serious doubts about, but both sets of parents were most insistent that all would be fine.

While there, I was introduced into English funeral practices. We had 130 funerals the first year I was there which kept the clergy and lay ministers extra busy on top of all our other duties.

There was seldom a wake as in the U.S. I would meet the grieving family a few days before the funeral to plan the service, and offer what comfort I could. I would say that 90% of the services I took were at the local crematorium. The celebrant was only allowed twenty five minutes, such was the heavy schedule for funerals at the crematorium. It was not easy fitting two hymns (selected by the family), a reading, prayers and a homily into that time frame. Once I went a couple of minutes over and the manager of the crematorium was frantically waving his arms at the back of the room wanting me to conclude. A few of the funerals were in the church, with burial in the churchyard which was much more dignified.

As part of the Established Church we were required to take the burial if the family requested it, even if the person had never or seldom been to church. I always looked on it as an opportunity to serve a family in their need. When a funeral was held in the crematorium the family would usually pick the music for the service. Apparently it was the wish of one deceased person the song "Wish Me Luck As You Wave Goodbye" be included. Not a usual selection.

In Neston/Corsham with a smaller population, we had around 80 funerals annually. However, the crematorium was much further away and I was often nervous at not getting there on time.

It was a privilege to be present with a grieving family. At 28 years, I first found this quite daunting, especially when the death had been a young person, or in some tragedy. Words do not come easily, but I began to realize that just being there was a comfort to those grieving their loss. More comforting words can come when the family is less in shock in a follow up visit. I would also give them a very helpful booklet "When Death has Touched Your Life" containing appropriate thoughts and prayers.

In Australia the service was usually held in a church or funeral home. Rarely was there a wake for Anglicans, and burial was the usual practice.

On coming to the United States I was in for some surprises. The wake was the usual practice, and an open casket was quite common. I had never seen a deceased person in a casket in the service before and I was caught by surprise in my first service in the U.S.

When I went to Scituate I had to officiate at some very sad funerals of young children and high school students killed in automobile accidents.

During my 18 month time in England, we had made many friends with whom we still keep in touch. We were given a rousing farewell in the church and presented with a handsome clock, a painting of the church and other memorabilia.

## BACK AT CHRIST CHURCH

After a few months in Marshfield, Simon invited me to return to Christ Church for a further 6 months. I was happy to accept and so was to resume where I had left off. The Curate's home was now occupied by the Treasurer, and was later sold, so I lived the life of a gypsy. Five different parishioners opened their homes for me to stay.

Fortunately I had only 2 suitcases with me, as I moved from place to place. My hosts were incredibly hospitable.

I would quite often eat out. One evening I decided to try a local Indian restaurant. I noted that I was the only diner. After being seated, I gave my order. When it arrived I began to eat. I noticed a local paper on the table next to me, being alone, I thought I would peruse it while I ate. On the front page was an article and photo that immediately caught my attention. It was captioned "Worst Kitchen Ever Seen in Swindon" It was the kitchen of the restaurant I was eating at, and it was truly gross. I got up as quickly as I could, paid my bill and left the rest of my meal on the table. Why they would ever leave that paper on the table way beyond me? Fortunately I suffered no ill effects.

The six months was up and time to leave. I had told Simon no farewell gifts as I had been showered with them my last time.

## NESTON

So I returned once again to our home in Marshfield. Soon after I was contacted by the Bishop of Swindon, Lee Rayfield, a former trained biologist whom impressed me as a pastoral, compassionate and highly intelligent man. He offered me a Curacy in a team ministry in the market town of Corsham in Wiltshire. There were five churches all together including Corsham. There was Gastard, Lacock, Bowden Hill and Neston. All small villages. The Vicar, Canon Roger Clifton, Rev. Sally Wheeler and I made up the team. We were assisted by some dedicated lay readers and a retired Bishop John. I was to live in the delightful small village of Neston, which had no shops or post office but it had a pub with an excellent chef. I would often eat at the pub and there met many of the locals who had no church connection. The vicarage was a modern four bedroom bungalow set in a quiet country lane next to the church. As of course, I had no furniture, the parishioners graciously furnished me with two beds, a lounge suite, dining table and chairs, a stove, washing machine (supplied by the Bishop), kitchen and household necessities and even a TV. I had everything I needed thanks to the kindness of the parishioners. I thoroughly enjoyed English village life, and the villagers were very hospitable. Again, Joan would come for a few weeks before returning to babysitting the grandchildren.

With five churches to care for, Roger, Sally and I were kept very busy. Once again I was a "house for duty" priest, no stipend, but housing and fees. The three of us took turns on Sundays at each one of the churches. Roger and Sally were superb colleagues, and it was a joy to work with them. All five churches were different. Neston where I lived, the church was built in 1856, attractive, on the small side with a graveyard separating it from the vicarage. It had a small but faithful congregation, and I soon became fast friends with Steve Drew, the Senior Warden and his wife Gill, as well with Lady Mary Fuller who was the widow of the former Lord of the Manor, and lived in a delightful cottage in the village. In 2017 she celebrated her 100th birthday, still "sharp as a tack", and still driving, at 101 years olds.

Corsham was the main centre of the ministry. A pleasant market town, a few miles from Bath, and where I would do my shopping. It also had several nice pubs. The Church of St. Bartholomew was a magnificent 13th century gothic edifice with a soaring spire and inside were tombs of medieval notables. I often had goose bumps when I celebrated the Eucharist, remembering how for centuries the holy communion service in all its various forms had taken place right here. The continuity of the church's worship of God over the centuries and the communion of saints became very real to me. The congregation here was the largest and had a fine choir.

Again, I made many friends. The men's group met at a local pub with lots of merriment and interesting speakers.

In the town of Corsham, there is a huge country house of nearly 100 rooms called "Corsham Court" It has lovely gardens, where peacocks roam freely. Built in 1582, it houses picture galleries with many masterpieces. On my first of many visits, I spotted a gentleman standing by a desk. Presuming to be a guide, I asked him where to begin my tour, where to find such and such. I finally said to him "How long have you been a guide here?" He replied "I am the owner of this place". He was the lord of the manor. Talk about being embarrassed, as I shuffled off.

The ancient village of Lacock was a picturesque place. It was given to the National Trust which of course meant it was to be preserved in perpetuity. Here was filmed Jane Austen's "Pride and Prejudice", and Judy Dentch starred in "Emma", as the village was the perfect backdrop for these masterpieces. There is also an ancient convent, secularized at the time of Henry VIII, and now a museum dedicated to a 19th century pioneer of photography.

The church in Lacock is another beautiful Gothic 13th century building dedicated to an obscure Saint Cyriac with a lovely interior. A plaque lists all the Vicars by name and going back to the first in the year 1200 A.D. It had a choir and faithful congregation who possessed an ancient chalice, never used, and worth well over a million pounds. The church badly needed a new roof, even so, some villagers unsuccessfully sought to block its sale. Strange how humans can be so illogically obstinate.

The wife of the Prince of Wales, Camilla, lived nearby and some of her family were married in the church. One Sunday I was invited by Camilla for lunch and I happened to say at the coffee hour that I had been invited by Camilla for lunch. "How on earth did you get such an invitation?" was the astonished reaction. Much laughter when I explained it was not the royal Camilla, but a parishioner also named Camilla. Sarah my colleague told me how she once officiated at the wedding of one of the royal Camilla's sons, attended by some members of the royal family (not the Queen) and how she enjoyed telling them to "sit" and "stand" during the service.

The Church of Bowden Hill was built by the brother of William Gladstone, the Prime Minister in thanksgiving for the birth of his son. He had daughters as well, it's not recorded what they thought of it. It is a 19th century building with a tiny congregation and it is hard for me to see how it could survive.

The fifth congregation is in the village of a Gastard. It is a small 19th century building with a very faithful older congregation who are close knit and caring. I was many times invited to their homes and it was always enjoyable to be with them.

The Wilshire countryside is very attractive, green hills and meadows with fields of grazing sheep and cattle, narrow lanes with hedgerows on either side which meant you had to drive with caution and at times ready to backup to allow another car coming in the opposite direction to go by. I loved the long summer evenings when at times it would not be dark until nearly 10 p.m. I enjoyed nothing better than in the quiet evening hours strolling down the country lanes, free of traffic with farm homes scattered along the way.

During the year I had in Neston, Mike Hayward, who owned a busy garage in Swindon, and who along with his wife Lucy, who I had become friends with while I was in Swindon, very generously loaned me a Rover automobile for free for the entire time I was in England. The dinner I treated them to at a very nice restaurant didn't even begin to cover their generosity. Another Swindon friend, Peter Ford took me to the Gower Peninsula in beautiful Wales, as well as to the interesting sights in Bristol and Somerset.

My Leighton wanderlust was really let loose in my days off from the parish duties. I traveled south to Christchurch to stay at the spacious waterfront home of Chris and Yvonne Savage, Scituate friends. They took me on an extensive tour of the well known and lovely Isle of Wight.

Then on my next break to Norwich in the northeast, with its magnificent cathedral, and on further to the shrine of the Blessed Virgin Mary in Walsingham, shared by Anglicans and Roman Catholics and visited by countless pilgrims. A visit to the ruins of Glastonbury Abby, which even in its ruined state, was magnificent.

I always enjoyed attending evensong in the cathedrals I visited. For me it was a beautiful, spiritual experience, the music sung by the superb men and boys choir, the gorgeous surrounding architecture, the prayers and readings in faultless English and being seated in the choir stalls, which increased the sense of intimacy with the sacred.

Back in Neston vicarage I think Joan was surprised that I had even begun to cook some of my meals in a trusty cooker I bought, as well as washing and ironing my clothes and doing household chores. I realized that I had been spoiled in this regard. Hey, you either learn to do it, or you starve and look like a bum. Not to say that I was not a worthy patron of the fish and chip and pie shops. There was no laundry within miles so once again a kind soul came to my rescue with a second hand washer and dryer.

A new Curate was scheduled to move into the vicarage with his family that July, so my time regretfully was now up, and there were many fond farewells at the 5 churches.

It was time to settle down in our home in Marshfield. Although I still kept busy with services, at neighboring towns of Cohasset, Duxbury, Whitman and Braintree for vacationing clergy. There were many requests from my former parishioners at St. Luke's to give the eulogy at the services for their loved ones, as well as conduct the weddings of their children I guess clergy are like the old fire horse, when the bell rings we respond.

## MORE TRAVEL

For whatever reason I had developed a passion for travel. While quite young I spent hours with an atlas memorizing the capitals of the world's countries, and in the case of the United States, the name of each of the states and even many of their capitals.

Traveling especially overseas seems to be innate in the Australian psyche, maybe because of the relative remoteness of the continent of Australia to the rest of the world. Wherever I traveled overseas I would inevitably bump into an Australian tourist. The fact that Australia gives three months paid long service leave to its workers and a month vacation certainly helps. I admit that before I went to the U.S.A. I had not traveled extensively in my home country. I was to make up for that on my many later visits Down Under.

Everyone I believe, finances and health permitting, needs to travel. It is a broadening experience, gives one an appreciation for other cultures and peoples, their history and the often spectacular beauty of their land. It helps us to breakdown our prejudices, and leads to a better understanding of our world, and the peoples and cultures who inhabit it.

St. Luke's provided me with four weeks of vacation time each summer which provided us with the opportunity to make exchanges, and for trips back to Australia to visit family as well as other overseas adventures. Joan's airline passes were invaluable as in no way could we have afforded to go on so many trips.

Traveling back to Australia from the west coast of course you need your passport. I usually had to catch a very early flight out of Boston, in this case to Seattle. It was dark when I grabbed my passport from the bureau drawer before setting off.

After an uneventful flight to Seattle, I caught a bus to Vancouver, from where I was to fly to Sydney. Approaching the Canadian border, the driver said take out your passport. I reached into my pocket for mine, and to my horror, I had brought Joan's passport by mistake. At the border the agent said "You can come into Canada but they won't let you into Australia without a passport."

I made a frantic call to Joan, while I sat in a Vancouver hotel, who sent it over in 2 days, by good old Federal Express. In the meantime I took a ferry to Victoria, on Vancouver Island. A truly beautiful place, with glorious gardens. My passport arrived, and I was on my way again.

# NEW ZEALAND

I had always wanted to visit New Zealand at length, as before it was usually as a stopover. My opportunity came in November of 2010. I rented a Nissan Sentra outside of Auckland for six days and proceeded to drive north on the north island to the beautiful Bay of Islands. The scenery is breathtaking with many islands set in azure waters. I could have stayed longer, but there was much else to see. New Zealand roads are excellent and I encountered very little traffic. I next visited Waitangi, where the treaty between the Maoris and the British was signed, after a time of bitter warfare. The Treaty house is set amongst lovely grounds overlooking the ocean. Then on to Napier through a beautiful mountain range along a very windy road with many grazing sheep and cattle and only scattered farmsteads. I had hoped to cover even more of the North Island, but it is larger than I anticipated and I had lingered over the awesome places I had seen. I reluctantly boarded a plane to Sydney.

Then in 2013 after visiting family and friends in Australia with Joan, who had to be back in the U.S.A., I arranged to visit New Zealand's South Island. Virgin Airways carried me into Christchurch. Christchurch was still recovering from a devastating earthquake two years previously, which had cost many lives. Property damage was also extensive. The historic Anglican Cathedral in the town centre was so severely damaged it could never be used again. Plans were in the works to build a replacement.

I rented a Toyota Yaris and set off on the Southern Road to Dunedin, a city founded by Scottish emigrants. A splendid city surrounded by lovely countryside, especially the Otago Peninsula, and possessing an impressive Anglican Cathedral. Next on to Invercargill, on my way to Milford Sound. Left-side driving wasn't bothering me, as I had passed my driver's license in Melbourne on that side.

Milford Sound is a world heritage site, and I could immediately see why with its spectacular fjords, mountains and lakes. It is rather isolated and has no hotels to speak of. There was a camp site with cabins. The cabins were more like a metal kennel. Room enough for a single bed, tiny table, no toilet, mirror, TV or phone. The bathroom was some 25 yards from your cabin. All good for the soul and for $75. I took a delightful ferry ride through the fiord. Leaving there, I headed for the scenic city of Queenstown, located on a pretty lake, surrounded by mountains. At an earlier age, I could have made it my home, as a resident invited me to do.

I finally made my way back through the mountains and plains to Christchurch airport, having been blessed with dry warm weather, for the entire journey.

## ENGLAND WITH FAMILY

In 2014 as their Christmas present, Joan and I took our 3 children and five grandchildren for a farm holiday outside of Bath, England. It turned out to be a most enjoyable time with all of us comfortably accommodated in what used to be the barn. There was even a swimming pool, much loved by the grandchildren. It was a working sheep and cattle farm, a nice sampling of English country life. We spent time visiting the historic city of Bath, dining at local pubs, entertaining Swindon church parishioners and having Lois and Jessica Berry join us. Everyone visited London before flying back to Boston. "Can we do this again?" they all said.

## ENGLAND YET AGAIN

In October 2016, in which I said was my last visit to England, I recruited my Australian niece Sue Leighton to be my chauffer. Joan who had fractured her pelvis several months ago, although better, felt she would not be up to the walking. She did not feel comfortable with my driving on the left side in England, hence my recruiting of Sue. I was able to return to Christ Church Swindon where I had previously served, to visit with the Vicar, Simon Stevenette and his family and the many friends I had made. Simon graciously invited me to celebrate the Eucharist at the main service. At Neston, a smaller church, where I had also served I was invited to give the homily. It was truly delightful to meet up with them all again. Sue had gone off touring during this time. After this we traveled through the lovely Welsh countryside to the seaside town of Llandow, near Caernarvon Castle, a place I had never heard of but turned out to be a very pleasant holiday place. After visiting the historic castle where the Prince of Wales was invested, we went on to the gorgeous Lake District with breathtaking scenery. I enjoyed visiting the poet William Wordsworth's cottage with a side trip to Hadrian's Wall. The spectacular highlands of Scotland was next, then going south to one of my favorite cities York with its immense, awesome York Minister.

Driving around this beautiful part of England, I noticed a sign "Sudeley Castle" which I recognized as the house of Queen Catherine Parr. She was the 6th and last wife of Henry VIII whom she had outlived. After Henry's death, she married Thomas Seymour, but tragically died shortly after childbirth. Her impressive tomb is in the castle's chapel. The castle itself is a treasure trove of artifacts and historical documents of Henry's rule. I spent an interesting afternoon poring over them. The castle gardens alone are worth a visit. Our last stop was in the beautiful Cotswolds before Sue caught her flight back to Brisbane and me to Boston.

The odometer showed that we (Sue) had driven 2,616 miles in 28 days. An astonishing number for such a small island.

## MORE OVERSEAS JOURNEYS

In 2006 Joan and I took a seven day cruise on the sailing ship "Star Flyer" from Athens around the Greek Mediterranean Islands. The ship holds only 300 passengers, ideal for us, as we dislike the mega ships with their thousands of passengers.

Star Flyer was quiet and peaceful, with amenities that were adequate for us. Because of its size we were able to become friends with some of the crew, who sometimes sat with us at dinner, as well as our fellow passengers. Before setting sail we had time in Athens to visit the Acropolis, the National Archeology Museum, the Presidential Palace, as well as just enjoying the city itself.

As we sailed around the Greek Islands, my college history lessons came to mind as we visited the island of Delos which was at one time the religious and political center of Greece. The gods, Zeus, Artimeus and Apollo all had temples here, which were now in ruins. Mykonos was our next port of call. It has an attractive town of white washed homes and churches surrounding the harbor. We then visited Patmos, where a large monastery, St. John, overlooks the harbor. There is a cave where the apostle is said to have written his Gospel and The Book of Revelation. You can see also, many jeweled crosses and lots of very ancient manuscripts, in his monastary. The many many steps required to reach the hilltop monastery were well worth it. Ephesus was our final call. It contains the ruins of large houses, stores, and an amphitheatre where Christians were thrown to the lions during the Roman times. St. Paul visited and wrote one of his letters to the church in Ephesus.

Our tour finished at Istanbul. A fascinating city filled with history and one of my favorites. We visited Hagia Sophia, once St. Sophiás before the Muslim conquest of Constantinople and which is now a museum. It has the third largest dome in the world. We also visited the beautiful Blue Mosque, and also the home of the Sultans, Topahapi Tabia which is surrounded by all types of buildings including a harem of three hundred Concubines. The next day we took a Turkish Airways flight back to New York.

## TOURS WITH THE NORBERGS AND FRIENDS

A group of Joan's airline friends under the leadership of Nancy and Eric Norberg began to organize annual week long trips mostly in Europe. The group usually comprised between 10 and 12 people, enough to fill a van or two cars. Joan went with them to a large villa in Tuscany (I was stuck at work).

Then the next trip in 2005 was on the sailing ship "Windsurf". Before we boarded, Eric rented a van and we drove to Cannes, best known for its film festival. Eric got us a room at a 5 star hotel normally renting at 400 Euros a night for 140 Euros, it was where many film stars stay. We traveled along the spectacular Riviera coast between mountains and sea to Monaco, home of Prince Ranier and the late Princess Grace. You have to pay to even enter the famous casino, so we passed on it.

Then back to board our ship in Marseilles, which holds 300 passengers, a very comfortable sailing ship. I stood on the bow as we left the harbor, absorbing the experience. A severe storm came upon us very quickly and when Joan and I came down to dinner only Nancy and Eric were there, the rest of our party stayed in their cabins overcome by sea sickness.

Our first port was Majorca, in the Balearic Islands very popular with the Brits and Europeans during their winter. It is a very attractive place. There is a massive cathedral started around 1300 AD with incredible stained glass windows. The island has a nice warm climate.

Our ship had five sails, but a motor as well, for when there is no wind. A great trip all around.

The next trip was in 2006 when we headed for the Dalmatian Coast in Croatia. We landed in Zagreb, the capital, and stayed at the Regent Hotel where guests such as Queen Elizabeth and Elizabeth Taylor had once stayed. I don't mean to be a name dropper! We set off in an eight seated van for our journey to our villa on the Dalmation Coast. It is a four bedroom stone villa with a spectacular view of the "Kanal", as they called the strait. When you divide the rent for a villa by eight it is really not that expensive. The next morning we caught a fast ferry to Dubrovnic. A guide showed us around this historic city built right on the Adriatic. We walked it's ancient walls, that had seen many a conqueror. During the breakup of Yugoslavia, Dubrovnic was heavily shelled but has been repaired.

On leaving our villa we drove to Split where the Emperor Diocletean built a palace in the 4th century in which to retire. On our way back to Zagreb we stopped at the truly magnificent Plitvick Jezera National Park. A ferry takes you across to a place of beautiful lakes filled with fish and several lovely waterfalls, all in a woodland setting. Our flight from Zagreb took us home from a lovely land.

In 2007 I rode the jump seat on British Airways the plane being full, to Athens where I was to meet up with Joan coming in from Boston. From there we took a bus to Piraeus, to board our ship Regent Lines "Navigator of the Seven Seas" for a seven day cruise in the Black Sea. It is a most comfortable ship, all cabins have balconies and everything on board is free, except for the shore excursions. We first traveled through the Bosphorus, after passing by Gallipoli, a place dear to the heart of every Australian and New Zealander because of the tragic landing of their troops in World War I. At Yalta in the Crimea we visited the palace where Churchill, Roosevelt and Stalin signed their agreement during World War II. Then on to Sebastopol the base of the Russian fleet and where the famous charge of the Light Brigade took place during the Crimean War.

After a visit to Odessa in the Ukraine, our cruise ended in Istanbul. We planned to stay there for a couple of days.

I discovered that I had left my toilet bag on the ship with my contact lenses and glasses in it. Eric and I managed to wangle our way aboard the ship just 15 minutes before it was due to sail away, and we got my bag back. After some more sightseeing in this fascinating city of Istanbul I flew back to London and Swindon where I was working.

Then in 2009 Joan and I took a bus from Corsham where I was working to Heathrow to catch a flight to Lisbon for a seven day cruise on the sailing ship "Windspirit". Fortunately we allowed a good amount of time to catch the bus to Heathrow. The bus was late arriving in Corsham, then it broke down on the road and we had to wait until another bus came by. Finally when we were nearly at the terminal, the police held us up as some sad soul had jumped off an airport bridge. We were still able to check in but with not much time to spare.

Lisbon proved to be an attractive city and we enjoyed the ambience. The first night on our ship there was a bad storm with 12 foot seas. Only four of our party of ten showed up for dinner. Joan and I somehow kept our appetites. Our first port of call was Casablanca in Morocco. Humphrey Bogart was too busy to see me! It is a bustling city of 3 1/4 million residents, with an incredible amount of traffic as it has no rail or subway facilities. From there we took a bus to Marrakesh, three hours away. An interesting ancient city, although its bazaar it is not as good as Istanbul's. A favorite of Winston Churchill who painted many of its scenes.

Reboarding our ship, we traveled on to Agadir which was completely destroyed by an earthquake in the 1970's and now rebuilt. Some forty of us from the ship went on a two hour camel ride. My camel was heavily pregnant and the saddle kept slipping and sliding me off. It was most uncomfortable and I think my last ever camel ride.

We docked at the island of Layarate in the Canary Islands, which is volcanic, although dormant. We then docked at Tennerife the most popular island. Renting our own small bus and guide we traveled around the island which had excellent roads (thanks to the E.U.) and many spacious lanes. We stayed at the quaint Hotel Quinta Rosa opposite the parish church, and we joined a procession on St. Cecilia's Day when they carried a statue of the saint through the streets of the town. We visited the interesting National Park containing larva from the volcanoes and with amazing views of the ocean. Leaving, we took an Iberia flight to Madrid. The U terminal is 30 minutes from where we were and three of our party's missed their flight to New York through dawdling. A very interesting trip all around.

## HOLLAND

While I was in England, Tommi Flynn and Jeremy Bangs invited me to come stay with them in Leyden in the Netherlands. I caught a taxi at 4:55 a.m. to Swindon Station and then to the London underground at Waterloo

Station. There I caught the Eurostar, the high speed train that goes under the English Channel. I didn't get seasick during the twenty minutes you are underwater! My train stopped in Brussels. I was like some others confused as to where to catch the Amsterdam train as there are no English signs. (Should we expect them). Sorting that out, I alighted at the Hague to catch yet another train to Leiden. Tommi and Jeremy were there to meet me. We started with a new experience for me, buying me a raw herring on a bun, quite nice.

Leiden is a very old university town with lots of canals and students riding bicycles everywhere. After a delicious dinner I returned to my lodgings as Tommi and Jeremy have only one bedroom in their apartment. I was staying in a restored old home built in 1425. My pretty Dutch landlady Thayar and her husband restore old homes to sell them.

Next day after we visited Tommi and Jeremy's Anglican church, where Tommi designed the needlework for the pew cushions. We then went to the "Panorama". This is a 360° painting of Leiden in the 1890's showing the fishing fleet, the town and scenes of the day. Well worth seeing. We wanted to see the Peace Palace but it was closed.

Jeremy is an expert on the Pilgrims, and as they left Leiden for America, he opened up a small museum in the town. My stay was an enjoyable time, and after saying goodbye I caught my train. The train passed Brussels Red Light district, where there were lines of shop fronts with young women sitting in the windows. The Eurostar took me home, once again under the channel.

## NORMANDY

In 2010 we were in Normandy with Joan's airline friends. We stayed at a beautiful old chateau with beautiful grounds and gardens. Because a dozen of us shared the expense the chateau proved to be quite affordable. Sometimes we would eat out, other times we all pitched in to provide our own meals.

We all wanted to visit the WWII D. Day beaches. Looking at Omaha Beach, we wondered at how the American landing could have succeeded even with the terrible loss of life. The row on row of white crosses and Star of David's was a poignant reminder to us of the tremendous sacrifice which was made here. We visited the museum which recounted in detail the events of that invasion.

We then traveled through the green Normandy countryside to the quaint seaside port of Honfleur, lunching there before we headed into the ancient city of Rouen to visit the massive, awesome cathedral. There is also a stain glass church which was erected to honor Joan of Arc who was martyred in this city.

# SWITZERLAND

In 2011 the airline group with Eric and Nancy Norberg planned a trip to Switzerland where we would stay for a week at a mansion on the lake in Montour. From the balcony we had a lovely view of the lake with the mountains in the distance. One day we caught a cog train up into the mountains. Spectacular scenery of mountains, lakes, meadows and homes. In the evening we were treated to a Swiss home meal at Kiris, friends of the Norbergs.

Another trip was made to the Olympic Village in Geneva followed by a visit to the Nestle Chocolate factory. Hard to resist their scrumptious samples.

A light show on the federal building in Bern was well worth a night visit. A car trip up into the mountains showcased the beautiful Swiss countryside and quaint villages.

Our stay ended, we traveled by the efficient train system to Geneva where we caught another flight to Frankfurt and then back to Boston.

Switzerland is a land of spectacular mountain scenery but frightfully expensive.

## RHINE RIVER

In June of 2012 our good friends Tammy and Bill Lickfield decided to take a cruise down the Rhine River on the "Avalon Vinia", a 130 passenger boat, and we decided to join them. We got the last two seats on Swiss Air to Zurich, where we stayed the night. We were awakened at 7 a.m. by the Lickfields who had flown all night on another flight. We loaned our bed to the tired couple and then later in the afternoon we were bused to Basel where our boat was moored.

Our first visit was Strasbourg, the capital of the European Union and a truly beautiful city. It had changed hands several times between the French and Germans in its history and is now French. The handsome buildings are French and German and there is a magnificent cathedral which contains a 17th century clock calendar where figures appear on the half hour.

In Mainz we walked to the Gutenberg Museum. We were shown his press. He did not invent printing but rather moveable type. It took three years for scribes to transcribe the Bible. Gutenberg could produce 280 copies in that time. St. Martin's Cathedral in Mainz is a Romanesque building built in the 11th century, well worth the visit. A special train took us to the music museum in Rudenheim containing fascinating musical contraptions, including one machine which played two violins together. Our guide played a score of them for us.

Our cruise took us past ruined castles, vineyards, forests and quaint villages. During our stop at Cologne we visited its magnificent cathedral. It took over 600 years to build, huge inside and out, and really awesome. Cologne was 80% destroyed during the World War II bombing, but the cathedral miraculously survived. The crew on our boat were courteous and helpful. Bill did a great job mimicking our German director.

The tour concluded in Amsterdam where we took a glass boat tour of the canals. The canals are lined with hundreds of house boats, as well as many tall buildings, where furniture has to be hoisted up to the upstairs apartments.

Tammy and Bill were great traveling companions, easy going and they even laughed at my jokes.

River cruising is often easier then ocean cruising. There are no waves, it is a much smoother journey, the interesting places are much closer to each other and you dock right at the place you are visiting.

## THE RHONE RIVER

Such was our enjoyment of our cruise with Tammy and Bill we decided on a follow up cruise down the Rhone River. Starting with the fine French city of Lyon.

Our destination was Marseilles, but first we passed through the beautiful French countryside. At Avignon we visited the huge Palace of the Popes. Home of the papacy during the Great Schism.

We also visited an ancient Roman viaduct, still in good shape that brought water to the thirsty city. Another memorable journey.

## TWO THOUSAND SEVENTEEN AND EIGHTEEN

Getting older as someone has said is not for sissies. You not only find yourself slowing down, but are also plagued by various illnesses.

Two Thousand and Seventeen and Eighteen were not my best years. Soon after Christmas, after a suspected heart attack, surgeons placed four stents in my heart artery. I had a wedding for Danielle and Matt of Duxbury, to take place at St. Luke's on December 30, before they were heading for work in London. I pleaded with the doctor's to let me out to do the service. Wisely they would not listen and so the bridge priest Billie Mae stepped in as my replacement.

On August 6, my G.P., Dr. Radden took one look at me and sent me by ambulance to South Shore Hospital. There I was tested on the treadmill. I failed badly, fainting right on the treadmill. Before going to the I.C.U., I again fainted in a bathroom. The nurses could hear me saying "Did I flush the toilet?" My mother taught me to always flush the toilet. Obviously I was delirious. I had a pacemaker inserted into my heart due to a very low heart rate.

Again, I was annoyed. I had booked a flight to London in September for three weeks visiting my English friends. As I had not made a full recovery, I had to change my flight to October 10. Of course, British Airways hit me up for an additional $300 for re-booking.

Janine and Carolyn traveled with me for the first five days before they had to get back to work. I believe their mission was to keep an eye on me. It was not a good start, as the first evening I slipped in the bathtub at St. Matthew's house in Westminster where I was staying and fell with a hard thump on my new pacemaker. The next morning I was taken by ambulance to St. Thomas' Hospital Emergency Room. I felt sorry for Janine and Carolyn who were to spend the whole of their first day in London in the hospital with me.

I can't say enough for the British National Health, who gave me an x-ray, CAT scan, EKG, pacemaker check and I was seen by four different physicians. "How much for my care?" I asked. "Nothing" they replied. I must admit I felt somewhat guilty at not being charged. I did send a contribution to their staff Christmas party when I returned home.

After this, I took the bus to Corsham where I stayed for 3 nights in the garden apartment of Steve and Gill Drew. While I was in Neston, a village where I lived for a year,

Lady Mary Fuller, the widow of the Lord of the Manor, invited me after a midweek service to come to her cottage for a glass of wine. "I will drive you there" she offered, and I accepted. Lady Mary will be one hundred and one years old on Boxing Day. She has all of her faculties and her driving is fine. She wisely doesn't go on the M Roads.

From Corsham, Steve drove to Swindon, where I stayed for five nights with the Vicar, Simon Stevenette and his wife Nicola. It was so enjoyable to meet up again with my English friends, and to spend some good times with them. I told them that this was the last time I would be in England. They responded "you said that the last time."

From Swindon I went by train to Salisbury. The train is a very comfortable way to travel in England but very expensive.

My room at Sarum College had an amazing view of Salisbury Cathedral, which has the tallest church spire in England. While I was waiting outside the cathedral to attend Evensong, the place was swarming with police and firemen. Apparently some idiot had tried to steal one of the three original copies of the Magna Carta, by breaking the glass with a hammer. They caught him.

Returning to London by train, I once again stayed at St. Matthew's house which is conveniently only a few blocks from Westminster Abbey. I went to the Abbey for evensong. It is special to sit behind the choir if you can.

It was quite full. The usher was directing me away to other seating when I thought I would give it a try. "I'm a retired priest over here from the U.S." His response "trying to pull rank on me are you father?" He seated me in the choir anyway.

After our first time in England we joined Trinity Church in Marshfield. Trinity is a small, quaint Church with an ageing congregation who are very warm and welcoming. We are ably led by its Rector, Father Noble Scheepers and our enthusiastic Deacon the Reverend Mary Beth Emerson.

Father Scheepers enlivens our Sunday worship with his excellent guitar playing and singing. It is a good place for us to be.

## FIRST TIME BACK IN AUSTRALIA

The first time we went back to Australia was in 1966, five years after we came to the U.S. Janine was only six months old and she weathered the 21 hours to Melbourne like a veteran traveler.

At our stop of in Honolulu, at this time Quantas flights stopped here to refuel before making the long haul across the Pacific. We stayed in a church facility, near the lovely Episcopal Cathedral. Of course we took the opportunity to check out Waikiki, and some of the other beautiful Hawaiian beaches. A trip to Pearl Harbor was a must as we wanted to see the U.S.S. Arizona Memorial, which had been sunk by the Japanese attack in 1941. We discovered that no children were permitted on the memorial, so what to do. An American woman standing by offered to hold Janine while we went to see the sunken ship. So we handed 6 month old Janine over to her and off we went. Trusting or just foolish? We would never do that again today. The memorial itself is very touching, with hundreds of sailors still entombed there.

We set off for Down Under. The flight was uneventful until several hours into the flight. The pilot came on to the intercom. He said I have some good news and bad news. Gulp! Because we have heavy head winds we will not have enough fuel to reach Melbourne. The good news is we can make a stop in Fiji to refuel. The bad news is that they are in the middle of a revolution, so you must sit on the plane. The good news again was that we were once again safely on our way to Melbourne.

After a pleasant two weeks of being entertained by family and friends on our first visit in five years I set off to return, leaving Joan and Janine with her parents. I decided to take the opportunity to do some touring on the way back. Firstly to India, via Manila and Hong Kong, where I stayed at the Imperial Hotel in New Delhi. Having always desired to see the Taj Mahal I caught a train to Agra. It was a culture shock to see hundreds of Indians on the platforms in New Delhi where they had spent the night as there was nowhere else they could afford to live. Some tourist attractions do not live up to their build up, but if anything the Taj is even more breathtaking than anyone could have expected. It was built by a grieving husband in tribute to his wife.

Next I flew to Cairo, Egypt. I must have picked up a bug in India, which threatened to interfere with my plans. However I was determined to visit the Pyramids of Giza. In order to confuse the pesky camel drivers who wanted me to ride a camel the 1/4 mile to the pyramids I pretended not to understand them despite trying me in English, French, German and Arabic. I was Hungarian that day. The pyramids and the Sphinx were more than worth a visit. That evening a guide took be back for a sound and light show on their history. Unfortunately it was in Arabic, but the lighting was well done.

From there I took a flight to Amman in Jordan. The reason being I could not get to the Holy Land from Egypt as Israel, Egypt and Jordan were still at war, although actual fighting had ceased. From Amman I took a bus, crossing the Allenby Bridge into the West Bank. The Palestinian people were friendly and hospitable. Jerusalem was divided at that time with Jordan occupying east Jerusalem and Israel the west. I had to walk across the border between the two armies, carrying my suitcase, nervously aware that heavily armed troops were watching as I entered Israel. War was to break out between the two countries months later and Israel was to capture all of Jerusalem and the West Bank.

I was able to visit some of the places where Our Lord had been, lived, died and resurrected. It was of course an awesome experience to see and pray at the places mentioned in the Bible. I was to see them again during my second visit, which I mention more extensively later.

Next I needed to get to Tel Aviv to catch a flight to Rome. My day of travel to get to Tel Aviv from Jerusalem was on the Jewish Sabbath, a Saturday. In Israel everything closes for the Sabbath, stores and public transportation. My only option was a glorified private pick up, which stopped every time a traveler hailed it. As you can imagine it took hours and it was not cheap. Arriving in Tel Aviv, I discovered to my dismay that the employees of TWA, my airline, had gone on strike. My search for a place to stay in the meantime yielded a small beachfront hotel. I have never felt so lonely during my stay in Tel Aviv, not knowing anyone, uncertain as to when I could leave, surrounded by people, true, but unfamiliar with the language or culture. Finally TWA started to fly again and I was on my way to Rome in a 707 with two passengers.

Rome, the eternal city, deserved far more than the couple of days I had. The Vatican, the glorious Sistine Chapel and the Coliseum were musts. Next Paris for a whirlwind stay. My flight to Paris took less than two hours on Alitalia. A former seminarian of mine, Michael Murray and his French wife, squired me to the Eiffel Tower, The Louvre, and Notre Dame Cathedral besides introducing me to frogs legs (ugh).

My room was at the Scribe Hotel which is quite centrally located in Paris. I note in my date book that it was $17 a day, plus breakfast. Quite expensive? Laughable today! The next morning I set off early to walk to Notre Dame Cathedral, walking along the bank of the Seine, with its outdoor art exhibits. As I entered, there was a mass going on in this magnificent ancient church. The stained glass is spectacular, especially the gorgeous rose window.

My seminarian at St. Luke's and his French wife had an apartment on the Rio de Massine, and tracking them down they invited me to lunch. Their former Abbe (R.C. priest) was also there. He could only speak French and I had only English so our hosts went back and forth translating for us. Michael and Elaine Murray then invited me back to go to dinner with them at 6 p.m.

In the meantime I went to the Louvre filled with great art and sculpture including the "Mona Lisa".

Returning to the Murrays we went out to a fine restaurant for a delicious meal which included a snail which I ate with great trepidation.

It is always a help to have someone you know who speaks the language and knows their way around. They then drove me around Paris which is floodlit at night, down the Champ de Elysse to the Latin Quarter. Next day before catching my plane to London, I set off for the

Eiffel Tower, taking the elevator to the second floor, for a view over the beautiful city.

Flying to London, I checked in at the Green Park Hotel. A morning tour took me to the House of Commons, Westminster Abby with its tombs of Britain's most famous historical figures down the ages. Then to Buckingham Palace to witness the Changing of the Guard. I then went on my own walking tour through Hyde Park to Trafalgar Square and Lord Nelson's Column. A middle-aged lady from Wales I encountered there said that I must be very wealthy to be traveling around the world. Not bloody likely, although I am very blessed. The underground in London is outstanding the way it quickly and reasonably comfortably moves the people of London and the millions of tourists about, and I always "minded the gap". It took me to the Tower of London where so many famous people were confined including Queen Elizabeth 1st, some of whom, like Henry VIII wives never came out alive. We were guided about by a very humorous and informative beefeater.

The Reverend Bert Neil, his wife and family were living at Warburg Cross outside London and he invited me to come stay. Bert was my Vicar in Melbourne when I was his seminarian. Bert was to go to Sale in Victoria where he founded Sale Grammar School and became its first headmaster. He later died tragically young.

They were kind hosts driving me through the quaint villages of Surrey, and then to Guildford Cathedral which is relatively new, full of light and a beautiful interior.

Leaving the Neils, I took the train to Canterbury and walked to its magnificent medieval Cathedral, the very heart of the worldwide Anglican Communion. I stayed for a service of Evensong sung by the boys' of the King's School. I was quite transported in spirit by the setting and the beautiful music.

Next I took the train to Oxford. A friend then drove me in his MG the 5 miles out of the city to Cuddeson College a High Church theological school. The students there were studying in preparation for ordination. I was introduced to the principal, who was later to become Archbishop of Canterbury. There was one American and one Aussie studying there among the 85 students. After the evening service of compline, I retired to my room. I thought I did, until two of the students, despite a rule of silence after compline, took me down to the village pub for a pint of bitter. Students are probably the same the world over.

Arriving back at Paddington I caught the underground to St. Paul's Cathedral, Christopher Wren's masterpiece. An amazing beautiful building, a magnificent dome, splendid altar with a tribute to Americans who died in WWII at the back. Not cluttered like the abbey, its huge tombs of Nelson, the Duke of Wellington, Wren and other notables are all down in the crypt. I liked the words on Wren's tomb "if you search for my work, look around you."

I returned to the Neil's to pick up my bag and we stayed up talking until after midnight. In the morning they drove me to Heathrow to catch the BOAC flight to Boston.

Arriving at Boston on September 2nd it had been an epic journey for me with experiences I would never forget.

## CONCLUSION

I conclude this memoir, not sure that anyone will take the time in this increasingly frantic world to read it.

I am so grateful for the long and interesting life the Lord has given me. A loyal wife, of 60 years, who has put up with my foibles and frequent travels. A clergyman's wife, living in the church owned rectory is not always a bed of roses.

Janine, Christopher and Carolyn have made us proud with their own accomplishments, but more so in the strength of their character. We were fortunate to add Bob Beal, Mike Spicer and Jann Leonard to our family over the years, who have become valued members of our common life.

Our five grandchildren, Douglas, Abigail, Samuel, Sarah and Charles have been a constant joy to us. We have watched with awe how they are moving so well through the stages of becoming compassionate, mature adults, with Doug at Clemson University, and Abby at Merrimack College, and Sam, Sarah and Charlie on the pathway. In July of 2019 Chris and Jann moved to Sonoma California. Our family now has spread across the entire United States.

As I reflect back, there have been so many people who were there for me from my humble beginnings in Richmond. From an aunt, uncle and grandmother who as a very young baby, took me into their home and brought me up in a safe and loving environment. To a headmaster who guided me to my first job. To clergy, who in my adolescence, nurtured an abiding faith in God, when I was really floundering. To a church couple who introduced me to Joan. To an American priest, who took me on, sight unseen, and had the foresight to make it possible for us to stay on in the U.S. For the countless parishioners in the eleven churches in which I served who became friends and who gave so much warm fellowship in the gospel, and to the priest and his family and parishioners who so warmly welcomed me to their church's in England. And for the many who I have not named in this memoir, you know who you are, and thank you.

I regret the times I have fallen short of my family, friends and God's expectations. My failures are mine alone, and I am humbled by their love and forgiveness.

A special thank you to Pam McCallum who has typed out several versions of this memoir, and guided me through the process of having it printed.

And to our dear Lord who is ever with me, loving and guiding me, and whose daily presence strengthened me, enabled me to carry out the ministry, he had so long ago called me to, knowing that any failures were mine alone, yet still forgiving and encouraging me to do better.
Thanks Be.

www.ingramcontent.com/pod-product-compliance
Lightning Source LLC
Chambersburg PA
CBHW070918160426
43193CB00011B/1506